LEARNING A LIVING

RADICAL INNOVATION IN EDUCATION FOR WORK

VALERIE HANNON,
SARAH GILLINSON
AND LEONIE SHANKS

PHOTOGRAPHS BY
REZA

Bloomsbury Qatar Foundation Publishing
Qatar Foundation
Villa 3 – Education City
PO Box 5825
Doha, Qatar
www.bqfp.com.qa

Bloomsbury Academic
An imprint of Bloomsbury Publishing Plc

50 Bedford Square   175 Fifth Avenue
London – WC1B 3DP   New York – NY 10010
UK   USA

www.bloomsbury.com

First published 2013
© Qatar Foundation, 2013

Valerie Hannon, Sarah Gillinson and Leonie Shanks have asserted
their right under the Copyright, Designs and Patents Act, 1988,
to be identified as Author of this work.

BQFP Hardback ISBN 978-99921-95-56-7
BQFP Paperback ISBN 978-99921-95-55-0
Bloomsbury Academic Paperback ISBN 978-17809-37-54-0

Cover and design by
DES SIGNES, Paris
Élise Muchir and Franklin Desclouds, assisted by Marin van Uhm
www.des-signes.fr

All photographs are by
© REZA
www.rezaphotography.org

British Library Cataloguing-in-Publication Data
A catalogue record for this book is available from the British Library.

Library of Congress Cataloging-in-Publication Data
A catalogue record for this book is available from the Library of Congress.

Printed and bound in Italy

Cover picture
Sir Fazle Hasan Abed, founder of BRAC and Laureate of the inaugural
WISE Prize for Education, 2011, with students at BRAC Primary School
in the Korail slum, Dhaka, Bangladesh.

CONTENTS

FOREWORD

H.E. Sheikh Abdulla bin Ali Al-Thani, Ph.D.,
Chairman of the World Innovation Summit for Education
(WISE); President of Hamad Bin Khalifa University;
and Vice President, Education, Qatar Foundation

The World Innovation Summit for Education (WISE) was established in 2009 in response to the conviction of Her Highness Sheikha Moza bint Nasser, Chairperson of Qatar Foundation, that education must be transformed if we are to meet our shared global challenges and give every human being the possibility of leading a fulfilling life.

During the current period of prolonged economic downturn the challenges are being felt ever more acutely, and this second WISE publication, highlighting innovative links between education and the world of work, is both topical and timely. Everywhere, education systems are too often failing to prepare young people adequately for a technology-driven, globalized economy, and millions are still deprived of an opportunity to acquire even the most basic skills to support themselves and their families. At the same time, economic and social changes mean that education must be a lifelong process, not confined to a formal classroom setting.

In researching this book we discovered, once again, that outstanding people around the world have devised and implemented successful solutions to the predicament. These very human stories paint a complex, diverse and fascinating picture of efforts to harmonize the relationships between individuals, work and society. Each story is determined by the circumstances of its location, but all involve an aspiration to find new ways of confronting contemporary challenges through education. The book identifies common factors that link these case studies and suggests general approaches that may be adopted, and adapted, by educators everywhere.

WISE exists above all to promote positive change, and it is my sincere hope that, by spotlighting these 'education heroes' and their innovative methods, readers will be inspired to make their own contribution to building the future of education.

**Students taking a break
at La Bastilla Technical
Agricultural School,
Jinotega, Nicaragua.**

ACKNOWLEDGEMENTS

Writing the WISE book has been an incredible journey, literally and figuratively. Visiting 15 inspiring projects around the world, from a radio station in rural Nigeria to personalised schools in North America, will influence our outlook and thinking for years to come. We would like to express our gratitude to all those people who made *Learning a Living* possible.

First and foremost, we must thank the people that we visited for their hospitality, and for being willing to give up considerable time and resources to make our visits worthwhile and informative. Thanks in particular go to: Jodi Pincus and her team at Rising Sun Energy Centre; Ingrid Imenez of the Synapses Institute; Markus Fischer and Rachel Dale at La Bastilla Technical Agricultural School; Professor Qingshi Zhu and Dr Li Xu at SUSTC; Yoshihiro Tatsuta, KC Chang and other representatives of the Silver Human Resource Centres; Dennis Littky and his colleagues at Big Picture Learning (The Met) in Providence USA; Willy Mathew and team at LoYAC; Mhammed Abbad Andaloussi, Al Jisr School-Business Partnerships; Mervi Jansson and Satu Jarvinen at InnoOmnia; Mayyada Abu-Jaber and Mohammad Al Ta'mari at JCEF; Biligiri Ranga at Infosys; Nnaemeka Ikegwonu and Emeka Lewechi from Smallholders Foundation; Harouna Karambiri, Mariam Sou and colleagues at 2iE; Pujarini Sen, Sumaiya Haque and many members of BRAC; and Mrs Joyce Dongotey-Padi (or Akumaa Mama Zimbi) at Mama Zimbi Foundation.

Thank you to the many people we interviewed for generously sharing your thoughts and experiences with us. Your stories are what make this book special.

Thanks for the help, support and hard work of indefatigable research assistant Jonny Mallinson, whose project management skills, tireless enthusiasm and in-depth research briefs helped move our project forward. Thanks also to intern Hannah Yusuf-George, who did a lot of the foundational work at the beginning of the project.

We have quoted and referenced a great many experts in this book, from writers and academics to education practitioners and social innovators, whose work and thinking helped us to shape our narrative. Thanks in particular to those who gave up their time to be interviewed. We hope that we have honoured your ideas.

Our loved ones tolerated our absences abroad and our absorbed preoccupation when we returned. We are deeply grateful for their forbearance and support. Thanks are due also to our colleagues at the Innovation Unit who – as ever – offered challenging and constructive feedback on our work and pushed us to make it as good as it could be.

And our thanks go to Her Highness Sheikha Moza bint Nasser, Chairperson of Qatar Foundation, and Dr Abdulla bin Ali Al-Thani, Chairman of WISE. The World Innovation Summit for Education (WISE) is an initiative of Qatar Foundation for Education, Science and Community Development and was launched in 2009 on the instigation of Her Highness. This book and all the work that flows from it would have been impossible without her commitment to leading the search for innovative education that effectively prepares learners for life and work in the 21st century.

Student at work on the coffee tree nursery, La Bastilla.

PREFACE

On every continent, innovators are rethinking how we organise learning for work in fast-changing conditions. What is emerging is a profound understanding that this is not a separate – or lesser – endeavour compared to self-actualisation, the transmission of culture, and the other goals usually cited for 'academic' learning. Rather, they are all part of a seamless, mutually reinforcing whole.

The curious apartheid of separate 'academic' and 'vocational' tracks, has been deeply detrimental and has contributed to the ills that afflict education systems worldwide. Innovators working in the space of learning for work are modeling teaching and learning that has implications for *all* education policy and practice. This book sets out a picture of how such brilliant innovators, around the globe, are transforming the way we learn to support ourselves on this planet. It is about a fundamental disconnect and dysfunction between the worlds of work and education. But fundamentally it is about hope, success and human creativity. Starting with an analysis of how the worlds of work are changing and how workforces are changing too – in their characteristics, demands, needs and aspirations – we then look at the work of 15 innovative programmes in order to see how education also needs to change.

The selected programmes were generated through desk research, reviews, publications and through the WISE community networks, including winners of the WISE Awards. Whilst no claims can be made for representativeness, the programmes offer a glimpse of the diversity and range of innovation that is occurring in this space. They show new directions for the focus of learning.

And not before time. The urgency of changing how societies prepare and develop those upon whom prosperity depends is everywhere apparent. This book seeks to do justice to the work of those at the forefront of change.

**Arriving in Nicaragua,
on the way to La Bastilla.**

Al Jisr School-Business Partnerships
Casablanca, Morocco

Big Picture Learning
Providence, USA

Rising Sun Energy Centre
California, USA

La Bastilla Technical
Agricultural School
Jinotega, Nicaragua

2iE
Ouagadougou, Burkina Faso

Widows' Alliance Network (WANE)
Accra, Ghana

Smallholder Farmers Rural Radio
Owerri, Nigeria

Lumiar Schools
Sao Paulo, Brazil

**THE 15 PROGRAMMES
FEATURED IN THIS BOOK**

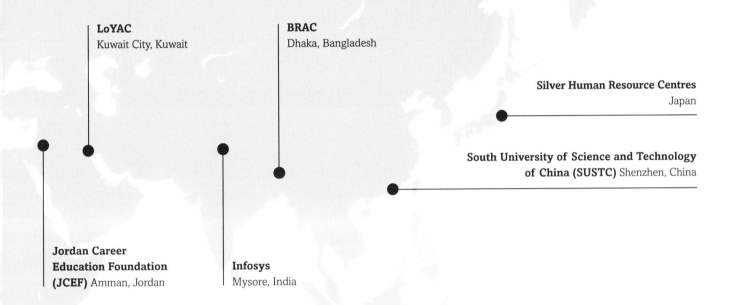

InnoOmnia
Espoo, Finland

LoYAC
Kuwait City, Kuwait

BRAC
Dhaka, Bangladesh

Silver Human Resource Centres
Japan

South University of Science and Technology of China (SUSTC) Shenzhen, China

Jordan Career Education Foundation (JCEF) Amman, Jordan

Infosys
Mysore, India

Danilo Yahn Zaidman benefits
from outdoor learning
at a Lumiar primary school,
São Paolo.

A pre-school plant
project at Lumiar School,
São Paolo, Brazil.

Students collaborating in the iGEM (International Genetically Engineered Machine) competition, at SUSTC, China.

CHAPTER 1

WAKING UP TO A NEW WORLD

How work and workforces are changing in the 21st century

I want to do something that I'm interested in. I want to pursue my passions and live happily.

Qijia Cheng
Student, 17, at SUSTC, China

China is getting rich now. But if you look at the picture more closely, you see that China is very unequal. So – how do we make society more equal? How do we divide the cake? It's up to my generation to think about these things.

Minghao He
Student, 19, at SUSTC

All my life I have wanted to go the normal way. But when I saw the advertisement for SUSTC I felt it was the right thing for me. Of course there was a risk that friends, family and society would not approve of my decision. And in fact my parents did advise me not to come – they felt that it was too big a risk – but they will support me whatever I decide to do. I'm glad I made this decision. [Here at SUSTC] we're like a big family.

Chenchen Lu
Student, 19, at SUSTC

At the South University of Science and Technology (SUSTC) in Shenzhen, China, a sense of excitement and adventure unites faculty and students alike. Temporarily based on an abandoned campus that formerly belonged to Nankai University, SUSTC opened its doors to its first cohort of 45 undergraduates in March 2011. 'It's like in the past, when settlers gave up the comfort of a known place and moved to unfamiliar territory,' says Professor David Shuk-yin Tong, who taught the very first lecture at SUSTC. Having worked for 25 years at the University of Wisconsin and then served as executive Vice President of the City University of Hong Kong, he speaks perfect English with an American accent. Many of the professors at SUSTC built successful academic careers abroad. They are not the pioneers of new lands, but rather are returning to their changed homeland armed with experience and confidence to play a role in transforming China's future.

In recent years, China's economy – the so-called 'workshop of the world' – has begun to falter. With workers increasingly demanding better pay and conditions, labour costs are on the rise. In 2011 the average wage for a factory shop-floor worker in China's Christmas goods industry jumped by 30 percent. This has led to the closure of thousands of factories as manufacturers take their businesses to cheaper South-East Asian countries like Vietnam. At the same time, the expansion of higher education has meant that thousands of educated graduates are flooding the market – 6.6 million college students graduated in 2011, up from 830,000 in 1998. [1] Levels of joblessness amongst these educated youth are high. Some are responding by heading abroad. Others are confronting the possibility that their future might not be as bright and prosperous as they had hoped. As *Time* journalist Hannah Beech puts it, 'How will a young generation weaned on double-digit growth rates come to terms with the disconnect between their exuberant expectations and the new economic reality?' Amidst all of this change and disillusion, different groups of society – from dissatisfied factory and farm workers to young people empowered by new tools such as social media – are demanding reform in every area: work, politics, education, and everyday life. [2]

SUSTC was developed as part of the Shenzhen authorities' strategy to transform the local economy from one that is predominantly based on manufacturing into China's Silicon Valley. Widely hailed as the country's most exciting educational experiment to date, SUSTC's mission is to lead educational reform within China's higher education system and to build a cutting-edge university capable of attracting and developing the world's best minds. It seeks to recruit students who are passionate learners and creative, independent thinkers, and as part of this objective it has – amongst other radical moves – worked with the Ministry of Education to develop its own admissions procedure. This allows SUSTC to select students on the basis of a range of competencies, not just on their ability to perform well in the country's standardised national college entrance exams. Deputy Director Dr Wei Han was part of the committee that set up the university. 'We're not trying to be revolutionary...' explains Dr Han, 'but we do want to play a leadership role in terms of culture change – to advocate certain values. And we want to educate talented people who can serve society, and make the world a better place.' This approach is reflected in the ambitions of the students, like 17-year-old Qijia Cheng from Beijing. 'When I was growing up I was always interested in cars – I wanted to be an engineer in the automobile industry,' he says. 'But since studying at SUSTC, I've changed my mind. And I've realised that the goal of my life is not just to be materially successful. It's also to be happy – and to do some good. I want to specialise in solar cells now. It feels to me like that's the future.'

SUSTC's emergence is a response to a world of work in flux. Myriad factors are shifting the work we do, how we do it, and who is doing it. As Qijia suggests, this has implications for more than economic growth – it creates the space to 'do something good' for the world.

TECHNOLOGY AND GLOBALISATION

It is widely acknowledged that technological advances are changing how we communicate, how products are made, and even how we think. We are in the throes of transition from an economy that relies primarily on investment in physical assets – buildings, machines and vehicles – to one where competitive advantage rests on investment in intangible assets – software and R&D, brands, knowledge and human capital. In other words, wealth is created these days when we 'bring together powerful computers and well-educated minds'. [3]

At the moment, neither developing nor advanced economies are keeping up. According to a study published in 2012 by the McKinsey Global Institute, by 2020 the world will have a *surplus* of up to 95 million low-skill workers and a *shortage* of up to 40 million college graduates. [4] This is not just about a mismatch of supply and demand – people fluent in technology are needed to shape the direction of knowledge economies.

Large multinational companies such as the oil and gas company ExxonMobil rely heavily on workers with science, technology, engineering and mathematics (STEM) skills to drive their business. ExxonMobil employs more than 18,000 scientists and engineers. Yet as Suzanne McCarron, President of the ExxonMobil Foundation, notes, 'Unfortunately, while the demand for STEM professionals is rapidly expanding, fewer students are choosing these important career tracks. [We] have made it a priority to support efforts to improve STEM educa-

Griselda Ruiz Hernández,
a student at La Bastilla
Technical Agricultural School,
Nicaragua.

Students carrying out an
energy assessment in Marin
County, California, USA.

tion by helping students and teachers pursue these important subjects.'

Work and workers are likely to look different in this global, hi-tech, knowledge economy. Workers will rapidly learn and change skill sets.[5]

They will work in ad hoc teams to tackle urgent issues.[6] They will be increasingly flexible – the internet and smart phones will blur traditional boundaries and encourage 'any time, anywhere' work.[7]

Globalisation and technology bring us together. The ability to work in global teams – with sensitivity to different cultural norms, and often in English – is in high demand. At SUSTC, students benefit from being taught by well-travelled professors who deliver lectures in English as well as Chinese, and who bring to their teaching a host of rich cultural experiences and international perspectives.

What these changes end up meaning is still very much up for grabs. For all those bemoaning technology that makes us all more antisocial, there are millions of people in Africa using their mobile phones to transfer money safely to their families. For all the worries of global homogeneity given expression at McDonalds or the Apple store, learning more easily about and from each other creates wonderful possibilities. As with all these trends, it is up to us to shape what kind of world emerges.

ENVIRONMENT

Our economies may be increasingly interconnected but our global environment always has been. The effects of climate change and the means of tackling them tie us all together. Our ability to collaborate and tackle complex problems, such as reducing carbon emissions, is central to the future of the globe.

In some regions, environmental shifts are destroying economies. Floods in Pakistan and Bangladesh and frequent drought in the Sahel mean that a productive economy is often a distant dream. According to the OECD, the increase in these natural disasters means that businesses in agriculture, insurance, forestry and energy will become unsustainable,[8] in addition to the direct impact on health and mortality. Often it will be developing countries, made vulnerable by geography and weak infrastructure, that will pay the highest price.

On the flip side, these shifts are giving rise to whole new industries.[9] The International Energy Association estimates that for every billion dollars invested in clean energy technology, 30,000 new jobs will be created.[10] Featured in Chapter 4 of this book, Rising Sun Energy Centre in California is a thriving organisation that creates green career pathways for young people and adults through offering training and employment opportunities related to energy efficiency.

ECONOMY

According to the International Labour Organisation nearly 75 million young people are unemployed around the world, an increase of more than 4 million since 2007. Youth unemployment is projected to remain at this level until 2016.[11] This has the potential to affect work and workers for years to come. The best predictor of future unemployment, research shows, is previous unemployment. Research from the US and the UK has found that youth unemployment leaves a 'wage scar' – young people earn less in middle age once they have been unemployed. The longer the period of unemployment, the bigger the effect.[12]

The other major losers in the recession are lower-skilled workers. In the US, unemployment is now 8.2 percent. According to the US Department of Labor, the unemployment rate for people in 'management, business and financial operations' is nowhere near this level, at only 3.8 percent. Lower skilled or manual occupations – such as 'transportation and material moving' (10.3 percent unemployment) and 'construction and extraction' (13 percent) – are experiencing the most severe economic pain.[13]

At the same time, employed adults are often keeping their jobs on different terms. Many are 'permatemps' – adults working permanently on a stream of temporary contracts because companies want a flexible labour force. In June 2012, the number of people in the US with temporary jobs had grown by 40 percent since 2009.[14] The ILO warns about deterioration of job protection laws in most countries. In developing countries up to 40 percent of workers are in the informal economy. Instability is replacing 'jobs for life' as the new normal.

What will it take for this latent labour force to be a source of sustainable growth, rather than of instability?

DEMOGRAPHY

Demography is contributing to changes both in the *demand* for labour and in its *supply*. In developing countries, high birth rates and relatively low life expectancy mean that the proportion of younger to older people is high. Young people in low-income countries in Africa make up 20 percent of the population. [15] In many Western countries, on the other hand, low birth rates and high life expectancies mean that the number of people in the world aged 60 or over is expected almost to triple in less than 50 years – from 668 million in 2005 to nearly 2.03 billion by 2050. [16] In Singapore the proportion of the population over the age of 50 is set to increase from 23 percent to 50 percent during the next 25 years. [17]

Where there is a vast majority of young people, the demand for jobs can be intense and frustrating. This is the case in Jordan, where the Jordan Career Education Foundation (JCEF) has formed partnerships to support excluded young people and help them secure local jobs; its methods are described in Chapter 3. Where there is a dominance of older people, greater productivity is required from the working population. There is also much discussion in advanced economies about the need for older people to work longer, and to be capable of retraining to contribute to new kinds of work. Established in the 1970s, the Silver Human Resource Centres in Japan are part of a nationwide, government-subsidised scheme that enables retirees to continue in part-time paid work.

A GLOBAL CHALLENGE

Taken as a whole, these factors paint a striking picture of a radically changing global economy, work and workforce. The nature of the change will depend on how we respond as individuals, organisations and as societies. The current period of flux represents a tremendous opportunity to shape a more dynamic, more sustainable and equitable world. However, without conscious effort it could just as easily lead to the opposite.

The innovators in this book are starting to produce the learners who are up to this task. To succeed as individuals and to help steer social and economic change, the featured innovations suggest that workers will need to be highly skilled in particular areas – from engineering and programming to languages and listening. They will need to be capable of deploying their skills with creativity and flexibility in different contexts and across disciplinary boundaries. They will need to be able to refresh their skill sets and work in new teams at top speed when required. They will need to be comfortable operating in multicultural and multilingual teams. They will need to be great communicators and interpersonal operators. They will need to be bold and confident enough to lead the way into new sectors and tackle new problems. They will need to be aware of and respond to the need for sustainable development. They will also need to have a sense of control over their own lives and a desire and capacity to influence the world around them – to help shape a new world as well as participate in it.

Data from employers around the world suggest that, at the moment, these people are just not emerging from education systems in sufficient numbers. 'In some countries, it's estimated that 80 percent of jobs in the next decade will require technical skills,' says Suzanne McCarron of ExxonMobil. According to Manpower's latest annual survey, 34 percent of employers worldwide say they are having trouble recruiting, with technicians, salespeople, skilled trades workers and engineers being the hardest to find. Of the senior Human Resources executives surveyed in the company's latest global annual survey, 46 percent said the talent gap was making it harder for their firm to implement its business strategy. Only 27 percent said they felt their business had the talent it needed. [18]

Confoundingly, these data are set against the backdrop of a world in which more people than ever are graduating from school and higher education. And in some countries up to 40 percent of workers report that their skills are underused. What they are learning is not necessarily equipping them for the world they are entering. Some analysts are warning of an education 'bubble' that is about to burst, and which could rival the financial lending bubble that exploded so dramatically in 2008. [19]

This leads to a seeming paradox. Education is both more necessary *and* more overrated than ever. Talal Abu Ghazaleh, who leads a major global organisation and is starting a high quality virtual university, TAG–UNI, does not see a paradox, just a mismatch: 'There is no unemployment problem,' he says. 'There is a mismatch between unemployment and employment demand. Give me one million people today who are knowledge workers, there is demand for them... in future, the only source of wealth after oil will be knowledge creation.'

By equipping people with the skills, knowledge and attitudes to adapt to and shape this new world – the education bubble can become an engine for positive change. It is a tall order but not impossible.

A water and sanitation project at 2iE university, Burkina Faso. Research projects at 2iE operate with partners from leading international academic institutions.

Team-building
at Infosys Leadership
Institute, Mysore, India.

Trainees at Infosys, Mysore.
Mornings are usually dedicated
to learning new content while
afternoons are for applied work.

An electrical engineering
project at the Solar
Engineering and Energy
Saving Lab, 2iE, Burkina Faso.

CHAPTER 2

THE THREE ELEMENTS

A new learning model

We have good skills in entrepreneurship (in Burkina Faso) because we have to. Life is hard. School eliminates these skills. It is our job (at 2iE) to help students come back to their talent, to dust off those skills.

Paul Ginies
Director General, 2iE, Burkina Faso

The cheering is deafening. It is standing room only. The winners smile shyly at the crowd but confidently wave their 1 million CFA prize money for 'best student business start-up'. Now in their seventh year, 2iE's Enterprise Days have been a roaring success.

2iE's Director General, Paul Ginies, is well aware of the global change described in Chapter 1.

Enterprise Days are just one of the ways in which his university in Burkina Faso is responding. Africa's population will double over the next 30 years. [20] 'It is not enough to have engineers. We need people who can invent new things. We have to build a new kind of society and we want to help drive the motor of innovation that will get us there.'

This ambition is shared throughout the organisation. Students and staff alike tell the same story. 'I am here because I want to contribute to Africa's development in my field.' 'I want to be part of Africa's future.' 'Europe is a machine that has broken down – here I can really contribute to building a new world.' They come from all over the continent – from Mali, Congo, Cameroon, Gabon, Niger, Togo and increasingly from France and Canada too. More than 35 nationalities are represented among students and staff. '2iE is not Burkina Faso,' says Benedict, a Burkinabe student, 'it is Africa'.

In pursuit of this grand ambition, 2iE is **matching students' skills** with local, national and global demand, equipping them with the ability to **generate solutions**, and the courage and imagination to **create new possibilities** for themselves and for the continent. Throughout this book, innovators are doing the same. Traditional education may be churning out graduates without the skills, competencies or attitude to flourish in a fast-evolving world – but with these foci for learning, innovators from Ghana to Japan, and from Finland to Nicaragua, are successfully equipping people to operate in the new world of work and to help mould its direction.

At 2iE, the transition to this new learning model has happened quickly. 2iE has been around since Burkina Faso gained independence in the 1970s but it was only in 2005, after Paul Ginies took over as Director General, that significant changes gave 2iE its current form. With government agreement, 2iE became a public–private partnership. The university started charging students fees to attend – at a level affordable by middle class families, and with cheap loans available for those unable to pay. And the focus changed from academic engineering to real-life engineer-entrepreneurship. In the past six years, the institute has grown from 460 to 2670 students.

The foundation of 2iE's engineering–entrepreneurship curriculum is the highest quality training in water, sanitation and environmental engineering. It is the only African higher education institution to offer internationally accredited degrees. This is hugely important to its students and to its faculty. 'I know my degree will be valued anywhere,' says Kahitouo Hien – a student originally from a poor, rural Burkinabe village. These skills are of critical importance to the continent. One third of people living in sub-Saharan Africa do not have access to clean water, while two thirds do not have access to proper sanitation (toilets). [21]

But Africa does not just need engineers – it needs engineers who are capable of using their skills to change lives. So classes are focused on what it is like to be engineer. 'They're always asking us – what would you do if you were in the field?' says a student. Lecturers and professors are all engaged in doing real-world work so they can pass on their understanding of the competencies required. Research projects at 2iE always operate with partners from top international academic institutions, and often receive funding from private partners looking for marketable innovations in their field. In hydrology and water resources, NETAFIM, an international irrigation company provides partial funding, whilst professors from Montpellier IRD-Hydrosciences (France) and Federal Polytechnic School of Lausanne (Switzerland) help to craft the highest quality work. Paul Ginies recognises the potential tensions in this: 'Of course we cannot legislate for the motives of our partners… but we want our innovation to have impact, and they have the infrastructure to take things to scale.' Active corporate partnerships also make it much easier for students to do the high quality work placements that are an obligatory part of a 2iE degree.

Emmanuel, one of the few French students at 2iE, identifies another characteristic of graduates like him that employers seem to prefer: 'TOTAL, AREVA, they like the fact that we know different cultures.' In the increasingly globalised market for labour, 2iE's international student body is a major asset. Benedicte admits that this mix of backgrounds, languages and religions is not easy at the start. There is much to learn about each other. But, over time, students build mutual confidence and understanding. For Benedicte, the thought of entering a diverse, new environment now is 'not a problem'.

Developing a bilingual (English and French) training programme is a continuing challenge for 2iE. Traditionally, 2iE was a francophone school – the official language in Burkina Faso is French, like many of its neighbours. With increasing numbers of students from Anglophone countries (including Nigeria, Cameroon, Ethiopia and Ghana) and an appetite to recruit and operate internationally, Paul Ginies is clear that English is essential. This year 2iE made a major investment in language teaching facilities and it will no longer be possible to graduate without basic English fluency. In that list of skills for employability, English is increasingly near the top.

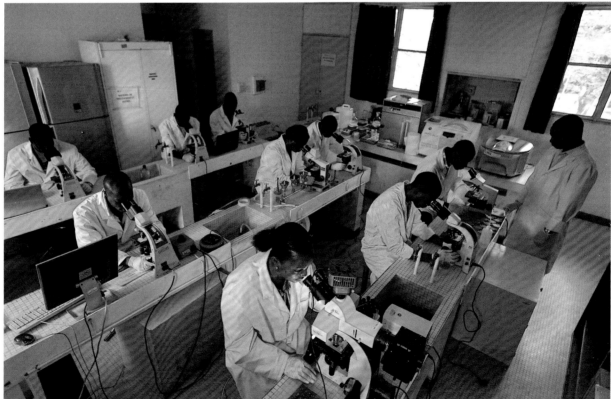

Testing vegetable oils in the Biomass Energy and Biofuels Lab, 2iE.

The Microbiology Lab at 2iE. In the past six years, 2iE has grown from 460 to 2670 students.

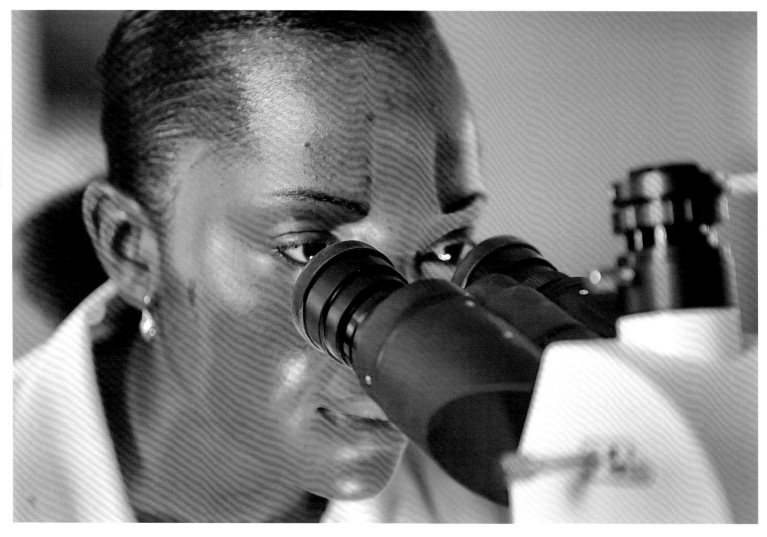

A PhD biology student
carrying out rsearch at 2iE,
Burkina Faso.

Up to this point, 2iE's story is impressive and relatively straightforward – their model is founded on developing relevant, high-level skills and the experience to apply them in practice. Unsurprisingly, 2iE graduates do not tend to have trouble finding a job: 95 percent have found work within six months of graduation and the remaining 5 percent are employed within a year. [22] Of the total number of graduates, 98 percent stay in Africa.

But really equipping young people like Kahitouo and Benedicte to fulfil their dream and 'contribute to Africa's development' requires at least two other major characteristics.

The first is independence of thought and problem-solving abilities. It is not enough to have a complete toolkit of skills and competencies if you do not have the flexibility to apply them to complex challenges – such as how to encourage local people to change their hygiene practices as well as provide them with the materials to do so.

Teaching at 2iE attempts to embed this independence and creativity in its graduates. Junior, a Canadian student, summed up how this feels different: 'In Canada, if I don't understand something and I ask a question of the teacher, they answer. They tell us what to expect on the final exam. But here it's different. Teachers say, "Go and look it up and find out for yourself." Or, "Ask a classmate." And anything could be on the final exam. You have to take responsibility for preparing.' Students are obliged to be highly proactive in their learning – filling in the gaps themselves, not as someone else has instructed them to.

'Junior enterprise' challenges help to exercise this problem-solving muscle. An optional part of the curriculum, 2iE's corporate partners set a real-life challenge for students to tackle. They also provide some resources. Students who take these on work in groups to research, prototype and construct a business plan for a new irrigation method or nutrition product. They are allocated a coach to help them. As Elodie Haniff, who leads Social and Environmental Responsibility of Enterprises at 2iE, puts it, 'They are engineers, they have loads of great ideas but they are naïve at the beginning. They need some extra tools to help them express their potential.' Their sponsors take many of these projects to market.

The final piece in the puzzle for Paul Ginies is the most complex. As well as having the skills, competencies and problem-solving abilities to tackle its existing challenges, 2iE students must have the ability to define and create new possibilities for Africa. Benedicte puts this beautifully as she reflects on her own experiences at 2iE: 'Now I am always asking questions. When I see a pile of rubbish by the side of the road, I ask, "Why does this happen? What can we do about it?" We have to find solutions.' For her, this attitude goes hand in hand with the revelation that 'You really have to go somewhere to see what life is like, to truly understand

people's problems'. She had always been interested in sanitation – but until she went and spent time in rural villages, she could not correctly diagnose the important issues. Her technical and problem-solving skills had to be connected with real understanding. Kahitouo adds the final ingredient: 'You have to dare to try.'

2iE provides learning experiences that attempt to enable all of its graduates to create new possibilities. This is where the engineer-entrepreneur model comes in: 23 percent of undergraduate lectures are in 'managerial sciences' with the rest in the technical disciplines described earlier. Enterprise Days provide the opportunity to test and show what this really means. In September 2011, students were invited to submit their ideas for social enterprises that would be financially self-sustaining, that would help to alleviate poverty and that would protect the environment. A total of 55 students did so, all of whom received expert support and coaching to develop their ideas. A final ten students entered the intensive development phase, of which five were chosen to compete in the grand final on 15 June 2012.

The competition was fierce. An insulating brick made of waste plastic competed with a paving stone made from discarded palm kernels and a water filtration system made of the sand that is so abundant in the Sahel. Each presented a ten-minute pitch to a packed auditorium and a highly experienced jury of professors and businesspeople. The judges pulled no punches – 'I can see a major hole in your business plan,' commented one. This rigour means that nascent enterprises are not just an educational exercise. 2iE has set up an incubator programme that helps take the most promising and most serious student enterprises to the next stage.

Kahitouo, global champion of the 2012 Berkeley Global Social Ventures competition, has an enterprise in the incubator. FasoProt aims to tackle the malnutrition so prevalent in Burkina Faso and elsewhere in sub-Saharan Africa. (26 percent of Burkinabe children under the age of 5 suffer from chronic malnutrition, contributing to an infant mortality rate of 9.3 percent.) [23] FasoProt will use an abundant resource that is sadly neglected in Kahitouo's opinion – highly nutritional shea caterpillars. Currently, women in rural villages discard thousands of shea caterpillars picked up in the process of collecting palm nuts for oil. Kahitouo has developed an efficient, low-cost way to turn the caterpillars into an enriched protein powder that can be used as a supplement, particularly for pregnant women, babies and young children. The potential market is huge and Kahitouo expects to reach 15,000 women in the first four years of operations. If he succeeds, he will simultaneously be tackling malnutrition and helping rural women to generate an income.

The incubator offers an initial investment as well as non-financial resources in an enterprise's founder or founders. Without this, Kahitouo would have to get a job. The entrepreneurs also receive legal, technical, managerial and research support along with help in raising funds. There are currently three enterprises in the 2iE incubator, with three more on the way. The intention in the long term is for 2iE to retain a stake in these social businesses, that will help to generate finances for the university as well as provide inspiration and role models for future students.

This incubator takes us full circle to the ambition that opened the chapter. If 2iE and its graduates are to play the role they crave in helping to shape a proud, successful Africa, they have to be able to create new possibilities, to invent their way to a new future.

The model created and illustrated by 2iE is not unique to its circumstances. The same three categories of learning have emerged as critical from other pioneers in this book, whether they operate in Finland, Nigeria, Brazil, Japan or Bangladesh.

The first is **matching skills**. In a world characterised by mobile labour, global competition and increasingly sophisticated technology, learning a living relies on the quality and relevance of skills and competencies. If mass, global education is not to echo the sub-prime mortgage bubble, such learning has to prepare students for the types of work that create value. It also has to equip them with the skills to operate effectively in the global workplace – from English, to mutual respect and understanding.

Generating solutions builds on relevant skills and knowledge – and asks for them to be applied to real-world problems. Where everyone can access knowledge and information (and with mobile phone penetration having reached 86 per cent by the end of 2011,[24] this is not an overstatement), and basic skills and competencies are universally available, then personal development, independence of thought and creativity start to take on a new importance. The application of skills cannot become the new factory line process. It is flexibility, collaboration and questioning that will enable people to solve real-world problems – and to distinguish themselves and their economies from the pack.

Creating new possibilities is about identifying which challenges and opportunities to tackle – to define the real-world problems that need solutions. It depends on authentic insights into people and context alongside personal commitment and leadership. Anil Gupta (founder of the Honey Bee Network and Professor at the Indian Institute of Management) suggests that in the future only 25-40 percent of our time will be spent working in a fixed place along traditional lines; the rest will be split between 'walking', observing the world and asking questions about what we are doing. We will spend 'less time doing things and more time deciding what to do and how to do it efficiently'. This will require greater personal agency – a sense of control and a belief that we can and should change things for ourselves and others – and closer connections between learning, life and work.

This book argues that these three elements should become the focus for learning that equips people for life and enables them to help shape their societies.

THE FUNDAMENTALS	THE BIGGER PICTURE	THE NEXT FRONTIER
Skills updating and matching	Generating solutions	Creating possibilities

LEARNING FOR LIFE: THREE KEY ELEMENTS

Ana and Moara share
a secret at Lumiar School,
São Paolo, Brazil.

Women building a pond
in a project initiated by 2iE,
Burkina Faso. 'You really have
to go somewhere to see what
life is like, to truly understand
people's problems.'

Members of the Hikpo
Widows Association working
on a pepper farm project,
Volta Region, Ghana.
The Widows Alliance Network
supports local widows'
groups to set up small
businesses, and provides
them with relevant training.

Audio-visual Communication students at the Omnia campus, Espoo, Finland. More post-16 students in Finland now choose vocational education than general education.

CHAPTER 3

THE FUNDAMENTALS

Matching and updating skills

Something interesting is happening in one of the most success-ful education systems in the world.

Finland has repeatedly topped most of the measures in PISA (Programme for International Student Assessment), provoking wides-pread international curiosity about the formula for its success. [25] Here is a system that elevates *equity* as its primary objective, not excellence (although it regularly achieves this too). In a small country with few natural resources, Finland depends upon its human resources to create prosperity. It has one of the lowest unemployment rates in Europe which it achieves with a high standard of living and excellent state-provided welfare, Nordic-style.

In such a context it is surprising to see what Sampo Suihko, deputy Mayor for Education in the City of Espoo, describes as 'a significant shift in thinking in Finnish society, especially amongst our young people'. Suihko was the founding Director of Omnia, an institution for vocational education and training (VET) with 10,000 students. The organisation he created with colleagues meets the VET needs of the populations of all ages of three cities: Espoo, Kirkkonummi and Kauniainen.

In Finland, at age 16, students who have completed 'basic education' choose either to pursue their education in General Upper Secondary schools (Gymnasia), which give a primarily academic education, or go to Vocational Upper Secondary Schools. In this well educated population, it is the vocational schools that are now more popular. Data from the Finnish Board of Education show that in 2010, 48 percent of the cohort chose the vocational route (up from 36 percent in 2001), whereas 47 percent chose the general academic route (down from 54 percent in 2001).

These data are reflected in the applications to Omnia between 2006 and 2012. Applicants who named the college as their first choice rose from 1500 to 2300. This is a steady year-on-year rise, not a spike. Sampo Suihko remarks: 'VET used to be seen as for losers. Affluent, highly educated parents would never dream that it was for their children. But now, with the competition for places, you have these parents phoning up and demanding to know why their kids couldn't get in! There's a new pride too. The brand has changed. "VET" used to be a pejorative term – not any more.'

What underlies this fascinating and encouraging turnaround? The struc-ture of Finnish education has helped – it models a flexibility that is rare. Choosing the vocational pathway does not constrain students in any sense. They can choose a dual track leading to both the matriculation certificate and a VET qualification. In any case, the three-year vocatio-nal upper secondary qualification includes a national core curriculum (maths, physics, chemistry, social studies, foreign languages), which gives them access to any university – both academic and applied. They

Teachers learming iPad skills in InnoOmnia's café, Espoo, Finland.

Annina Cederström, at o+m=g design, Espoo, Finland, part of the InnoOmnia network. Annina was a graduate of Omnia's Upper Secondary vocational programme. 'The experience here has helped us develop our business model and change our focus.'

Jouko Kivimetsä, professor of design and innovation, displaying products at InnoOmnia workshop.

will also have had a choice of 53 vocational upper secondary qualifications. And in Finland vocational qualifications are highly regarded by all, employers and students alike. Moreover such qualifications are essential to employment, in marked contrast to a number of other countries where they are seen as low value. In part this is a function of a close match between the higher order skills that the economy needs and the skills that are taught. The curriculum is not merely instrumental, limiting their outlook and preparing them simply to be 'compliant employees'. Citizenship and 'learning to learn' are a part of the national core curriculum.

At a May 2012 UNESCO conference,[26] 117 nations gathered to debate the issue of vocational and technical education. The inadequacy of many VET systems in helping to build dynamic, inclusive and greener societies attracted strong criticism. It is a sign of deep unease when the demand is not for expansion but for *transformation*. According to the World Bank, the most successful VET programmes have managed to encourage integration with general education. They have also managed to improve mobility between VET and higher education whilst incorporating workplace experience into the programme.[27] Finland's system demonstrates this mix and is showing how attractive it can be for learners. For young people considering their options, the vocational education route is not a dead end or a second-class choice.

Notwithstanding this sound basis, Omnia has set about intentionally innovating – transforming – the learning and teaching experience in VET. There is an economic driver. Whilst the last decade has been kind to Finland, its success has been closely tied to a small number of big enterprises such as Nokia, which is now faring poorly in the face of global competition and laying off workers (numbers of whom are turning to Omnia).

Three areas of innovation demand attention.

The first is the establishment of an innovation force within Omnia as a whole. This takes the shape of InnoOmnia, the brainchild of a team that Suihko affectionately calls 'the propeller heads'. InnoOmnia started work in August 2011. It is probably unique, but will undoubtedly be copied rapidly (it is already starting to attract international visitors). InnoOmnia acts as the development unit for Omnia as a whole, tackling its most intractable challenges and testing out new solutions. Its flagship work in helping to support Finland's entrepreneurs is explored in Chapter 5.

The second area of innovation is one in which InnoOmnia has already demonstrated profound impact. The organisation took on the task of working with staff to re-cast the Business and Administration programme for 16-19 year olds, a group that had the highest dropout rate at Omnia – a grisly 60 percent. The major change was to increase the proportion of work-based learning and to integrate it into the programme each week – increasing from Year 1 until in Year 3 it is full-time (with teacher support and monitoring). The programme also began to use mobile learning technologies: iPod Touches and iPads for a wide variety of purposes, including assessment. And assessment is flexible: depending on progress and prior experience, it can be completed well in advance of the nominal three years. To achieve this, teachers have made great strides. They have learned how to use cloud-based services and their own mobile devices in new ways. And they have understood that *all* those involved in the programme assume different roles at different times. Everyone is a teacher, and everyone is a learner.

InnoOmnia now wants to use these insights to disrupt and impact teacher training for VET across Finland. It has started to win tenders for VET teacher training and is offering 'bootcamps':

- Edupreneur Bootcamp focuses on project-based learning, student entrepreneurship models and entrepreneurial teaching methods

- Edutech Bootcamp is a blended learning programme – online and in person. Teachers collaborate through social media and cloud-based services to support learning and to create and share content

Finally, Omnia is innovating apprenticeship. Dating back to the Middle Ages, apprenticeship is perhaps the oldest formal means of acquiring work-related skills. It has endured because the central concept – the structured learning of accredited skills, whilst in a real job – incorporates the key ideas of practice-based learning and relevance to employers. In parts of Europe where it is strongest (Germany, the Netherlands, Austria) it is a highly regarded option. In Germany's system – seen by many as an exemplar – nearly two-thirds of schoolchildren undertake apprenticeships and a quarter of employers are involved. This 'dual system' is one where the costs of employment and tuition are met 50–50 by State and employers. It is a major factor behind Germany's relatively low rate of youth unemployment.

Finland already has a strong and unusual apprenticeship system – currently the majority (around 84 percent) of apprentices are over 25. The arrangement is seen as one more aspect of an overall strategy for lifelong learning. Allan Vilmunen, now a Product Support Specialist with Canon, is not atypical. He began his apprenticeship at 55. A telecoms engineer of many years experience, he took a programme to acquire a diploma in digital printing after discussion with his employer and the Omnia apprenticeship office. It took two and a half years, during which he remained employed by Canon, but the scheme paid all tuition and program costs. It covered all aspects of software, workflows, printing mechanics, and customer service. The qualification is highly valued, giving customers and his employer confidence in the level and quality of his skills. Was it worth it for him – even at this stage of his career?

'Oh, definitely. The college recognised my previous experience. There was really good use of media, video, lots of discussion. Good processes. The learning was well integrated with my work. Our company values loyalty, and also recognises that older workers have "tacit knowledge". It's all about valuing people. Now (at 59) I am taking another qualification through apprenticeship.'

Despite these strengths, the Finnish system still needs to change. The government believes that more employers should be involved. It has launched a campaign to encourage participation, focusing on the need for more placements for the 16–25-year-old age group. This is a hard sell when an apprenticeship contract is for 2–3 years. Companies are often wary about investing in a young person (who then acquires employment rights) in this open-ended way – what if they are not good enough? Omnia, naturally, is looking to innovate in this space. It is devising a '2+1' model for apprenticeship in which apprentices spend two years at Omnia (with work placements) and then one year employed full-time on a temporary contract. They believe this will be more attractive to risk-averse employers. Creating a more flexible apprenticeship system that maintains the guarantee of quality for trainees, whilst preserving options for employers, could significantly boost take-up. Mervi Jansson, Director of Learning Solutions, sees it as another instance of integration: 'We have to break down barriers. No boundaries! We have to get all things working together: theory, work, student support, financing models. You get a great skills-match – employers really know what is needed. This is good for employers – it can be a fantastic investment.'

So even in the highly successful Finnish system, the urge to innovate is strong. As much as 13 percent of young people are not in employment, education or training ('NEET'). This figure is comparatively low (17 percent across the EU as a whole, much higher in many countries) but it haunts this society that is so committed to equity. [28] And this level of disengagement persists despite the availability of the high quality vocational upper secondary school option to everyone. For some, the school framework just doesn't work. Hence the drive to design new models that are even more attractive and flexible and that provide a return on investment.

The effort will be of considerable interest to many governments, not least in Europe where the decade's disastrous impact on young people demands the invention of new models and approaches that attract wider employer and learner engagement. Italy and the UK have both announced revamped apprenticeship initiatives in 2012.

Underpinning all of Omnia's innovations is a coherent, modernised and profoundly human concept of learning and teaching. Consistent with the approach that made Finland's schooling system so successful, up-skilling the teaching force is central.

As Mervi Jansson puts it: 'Teachers need to see and experience how learning can be different, even within a framework of a national curriculum. Their repertoire needs to be extended to include mobile learning, cloud-based services, gamification – and of course, project-based learning. As teachers we need to take that crucial step into anytime and anywhere learning. When they do it, they get it. We say: challenge, engage, empower! The feedback and response from students is the most powerful driver for change. We are re-making a future here, one that can't be moved to China.'

––––––––––

The skills equation used to be conceived as relatively simple: employers created jobs and education systems produced the skilled workers to fill them. The task of education was therefore to create the foundation of basic skills and knowledge upon which more technical and vocational skills were built, and to provide formal opportunities to acquire and assess those technical and vocational skills. In the most successful economies, business and education collaborated closely on this match.

Now, as discussed in Chapter 1, it seems ever harder to get that balance right – even in contexts where there is high unemployment. Too often there is a mismatch between the skills needed by employers and those on offer by graduates. According to Deloitte, there were 3.2 million unfilled jobs in the USA as of July 2011. These shortages often occur in critical, skilled roles that have high barriers to entry and are crucial to a company's success. This skills mismatch arises in part through an undifferentiated national approach rather than a more localised one, and also through the practice of basing the funding of education providers on the number of qualifications obtained rather than job outcomes. Finland bases its funding for institutions on a formula that includes success in finding employment for graduating students.

But even in such a highly developed (and relatively small) system as Finland's, matching skills is difficult – there is the added complication of planning for the future needs of an economy in which key jobs have not yet been invented. ILO labour economist Raymond Torres is clear: 'In countries like Spain, where youth were encouraged to gain higher academic qualifications, disillusion and dismay is severe. They were encouraged to obtain qualifications in engineering and technical aspects of construction, and now the property bubble has burst. The big challenge is to find a better interaction between education and the labour market. But that cannot be about just simply following a view of "what the economy needs". There has to be a longer term view.' The OECD has sought to help through the publication of its Skills Strategy 2012 [29] with tools for local policy makers to identify a better match between skills and needs.

One way to bridge the gap – both between learners and employers, as well as between the present and the future – is to bring skills acquisition in-house. Some organisations are defining the jobs of the future and training their own staff to fill them.

EMERGING PROVIDERS: THE 'CORPORATE UNIVERSITY'

Infosys, India, is one such company. In 2012–13, it will hire 35,000 new employees, up to 20,000 of which will be trained at their Global Education Centre (GEC) in Mysore – a majestic campus 500 miles from Pune where the company was founded thirty years ago. It is not hard to believe in the declaration of Infosys' co-founder, Narayana Murthy: 'Our people are our biggest assets. At the end of the day, when everyone goes home, our assets go down to zero.' Evidence of the company's commitment to this mantra is visible everywhere at GEC – in the ex-military security on the gates, the manicured landscaping, the squash courts, swimming pool and multiplex cinema. Infosys is investing where it sees its future – in its employees' learning.

The rationale for such a luxurious environment is not just to make its employees feel valued. It is to enable trainees to focus entirely on learning without having to worry about anything else, says Dr Subraya, Head of the Global Education Centre. This forensic attention to detail in creating the perfect environment for learning has also been applied to the design of the training itself.

The genesis of the programme is now familiar – Infosys needs highly trained engineering graduates of all disciplines. These graduates are not hard to find in India's huge and aspiring middle classes who believe in the value of a high quality education. What is hard to find among these young people is the right skill set, disposition and discipline to operate in the new work place. Infosys' graduate training aims – very precisely – to bridge this gap.

Dr Subraya describes four key elements to the programme: practicality (the ability to apply knowledge and expertise); quality control (the ability to assess and maintain Infosys standards of excellence); behaviour (the ability to listen, present and be comfortable in a multicultural environment); and corporate values. For trainees, mornings are usually dedicated to learning new content while afternoons are about applied work – solving real-life challenges in groups. Siddharth says this is the biggest difference from college. 'The good thing is that concepts are always employed directly. You understand the significance of what you have learnt.' One sees here the direct linkage between 'academic' concepts and vocational/practical application.

GEC's trainers are constantly in the market place, testing and updating their assumptions about what is needed. This often includes new technical specialisms – mobile and cloud computing for example. Minor changes like these are made to the curriculum all the time – it is just a question of adding new modules. More profound changes take longer. Dr Subraya sees the next frontier being to transform their highly skilled software engineers into the 'whole package – effective project managers and businesspeople too'. This diligence seems to be paying off – the latest evaluation of trainees, 6-8 months into their placements, found that the training they received at GEC tallied 98.8 percent with the real-life demands of the work place.

Aleesha, a trainee, describes the experience as 'a great transformation… it has absolutely changed us. Infosys makes me believe I can do so much. It is the best thing that has happened to me.' This enthusiasm is particularly impressive in the context of Aleesha's daily routine. The campus may seem like paradise but the learning commitment does not make for an easy life. Trainees attend classes between 8:30 am and 6:00 pm each day. Every evening they do a self-assessment to check their understanding of the day's content. Then it is back to their rooms to download and prepare content for the next day. For 'green/high performers' the weekends are free to enjoy the many sports and cultural clubs on offer at the campus. For 'yellow/middle performers' Saturday may involve a full day of work to get up to speed on the week's modules. For 'red/low performers', the weekend is focused entirely on work.

The red–yellow–green traffic light system is understood and observed by students and teachers alike. Self-assessments are voluntary but 95–98 percent of students do them every day. Teachers observe the results and can follow up with individuals when they perceive a real problem – or with a whole class if it is obvious that there is a collective lack of understanding.

For Dr Subraya, this is a critical feature of the system: 'Learning does not happen in islands here… it all builds on itself, it is sequential.' Unlike at university, where you can pick and choose modules that may or may not relate to each other, here every module is a necessary step to understanding the next one. Without the self-assessment system, students could very quickly find themselves totally at sea. Of course, this progression could be enforced with teacher-led, obligatory testing. The voluntary element of this reflects a key value of the learning philosophy at Infosys. 'Trainees have to take responsibility for their own learning… they have to draw it down actively… we do not hand it to them on a plate.' Notwithstanding this level of learner ownership, the practical learning-by-doing is embedded in a highly structured pedagogy, in line with the research findings that advocate this approach.[30]

For Infosys, the investment in learning is huge and so is the return. All trainees are paid a salary during their time at GEC but no-one is obliged to stay – either during or after the training period. Less than 1 percent of trainees leave. On average, trainees choose to stay for 3-5 years – far longer than necessary for Infosys to recoup its investment. Many go on to higher degrees, and the door is always open for them to return after their studies.

––––––––––

Elsewhere in the world not-for-profits are showing the way to more meaningful skills acquisition. In developing countries with poorly performing education systems, social entrepreneurs are starting to make deep connections with business, which the formal education systems have failed to make. The innovation lies in being a skilled and strategic intermediary.

MATCHING SKILLS IN THE MIDDLE EAST

––––––––––

Ahmed Salem lives near the city of Ma'an in southern Jordan. The culture is Bedouin. There are few employment opportunities, little entertainment and lots of ill health. In a country where unemployment is chronic, the youth are hardest-hit: the unemployment rate amongst those under 24 is said to be 28 percent – but most people think it is higher. According to World Bank data, [31] the MENA region has one of the highest unemployment rates in the world, and the rate is at its highest for those with higher education degrees. The beginning of the Arab Spring was marked in Ma'an by riots, vandalism, and the threat of a general uprising. It was, as many have remarked, a wake-up call. Ahmed, like most of his friends, was unemployed – and had been so for over a year – when he had the good fortune to become involved with the Jordan Career Education Foundation (JCEF).

An NGO, JCEF is supported by the Washington-based Education for Employment philanthropic initiative, which operates across the Middle East. JCEF's mission is to reduce unemployment amongst Jordanians and establish a new generation of confident professional leaders.

JCEF's Chief Executive Mayyada Abu Jaber is one of those impatient innovators whose ideas are practical and who possess the drive and determination to develop them, irrespective of setbacks and gloom. Under her leadership, JCEF did not try to reinvent the wheel but adopted and adapted good practice from Education for Employment. JCEF utilised a number of their curricular and philosophical approaches. For Mayyada though, there were two key insights.

Ahmed was one of the first recruits. 'I was very angry a lot of the time. Very negative. I became depressed about my life, and I couldn't see any possibility of advancement.' Ahmed comes from a family of 11, in which there are only two members working – he and his brother. 'I learned a whole new set of skills I had no idea existed. I am so much less angry. I use my skills around conflict resolution with others too – my community, my family are asking "What happened?" Now, I'm telling my community about it. Also, I'm giving back: I'm offering free welding assistance to people who need little jobs done – and I'm telling other people to try to get into this.'

So, what happened? JCEF worked with MID to devise a recruitment and training strategy. They went to Ma'an and sought out 300 applications from the local market. They recruited a first cohort of 60 young men, rented a hangar at the Ma'an Industrial Zone and purchased welding machines. Their agreement with MID Contracting was to offer salaries, transportation and Social Security, plus the guarantee of work at company projects if the trainee passed. In return for this, recruits had to learn – sometimes from a very low base – how to be an employee and how to work with others, even before they acquired technical skills to 3G welding standards.

Faten Jabr is the Chief HR Manager for MID, where she has worked for many years. She is emphatic that so-called 'soft skills' are a vital platform for enabling young people from tough backgrounds, in high poverty, to be successful: 'Many of our recruits hadn't finished school (because of poverty). They may not even have finished sixth grade. We do require basic standards of literacy, but they have to learn how to operate in a workforce. They maybe have uneducated parents, and have no idea what a professional environment is like. They need to understand respect for each other, time management, how to listen with an open heart and an open mind. Basically to understand about the environment of work. JCEF did this really well. They created the technical programme too, to complement it, and then brought in a third party for the testing programme for 3G welding – to international standards. Now we're creating an advanced programme too – this is a big success story for us. We want to work with the local youth, we don't want to have to recruit abroad when there is such a problem here. We have a big commitment to Jordanian society – we're a Jordanian company.'

This approach to skills fits well with research findings. According to ILO labour economist Raymond Torres: 'People must now acquire the interpersonal skills which will enable them to change ways of working, routines and organisation – the contours of the enterprise. And people must acquire the skills to collaborate and work together as never before. There is plenty of training available in the acquisition of technical skills, but less training of the brain and in social interaction – and this needs to be researched and developed.'

Ahmed Saleh, one of the first
recruits to the Jordan
Career Education Foundation
training strategy.

Sereen Azmi selling fabrics
at Jabal Al-Qala'a, Jordan.
Trainees with the Jordan
Career Education Foundation
are supported to develop
self-confidence and take
responsibility.

JCEF's Chief Executive Mayyada Abu Jaber is one of those impatient innovators whose ideas are practical and who possess the drive and determination to develop them, irrespective of setbacks and gloom. Under her leadership, JCEF did not try to reinvent the wheel but adopted and adapted good practice from elsewhere. They are affiliated to Education for Employment, a regional non-profit that was founded in 2004 on the belief that if young people have satisfying jobs and hopes for their future, they will contribute to the development of secure and peaceful societies. JCEF utilised a number of their curricular and philosophical approaches. For Mayyada though, there were two key insights.

One was shifting focus from supply to demand: 'We try to get really close to what businesses need. We start with a needs analysis: what are your needs, which skills, what kind of headcount? We focus mainly on sectors that want at least 50 employees. The situation was mad, with high unemployment, and yet recruitment going on from abroad. We find there is a big gap between what employers want and what students get.'

The second insight was the proactive approach required if their mission to address the needs of the most disadvantaged was to be achieved: 'We *look* for them. The ones who can find us can probably find a job,' says Mayyada. 'We go to the 24 or so pockets of greatest poverty. We go into the cafes, onto the street, we connect with the community organisations.' Of course, these most challenged communities are less likely to make the numbers look good, especially as JCEF invites others to judge its success not on the numbers recruited, but on the retention rates within jobs. 'So yes, we have to stress commitment. Youth who understand this will work hard for themselves, not for the boss, and so can develop a work ethic. And therefore our emphasis is on "soft skills". You just have to put in place the foundations of understanding working with others and managing yourself. We know how to do that really well, in a way that empowers youth. They talk readily about self-confidence – where there was none; being prepared to develop yourself, take responsibility, not think you have to stop at a certain point.' The empowerment extends to offering the opportunity to JCEF 'graduates' to pay back – as Ahmed is trying to do in his community – by mentoring upcoming students, and by acting as peer advisors. This alumni network is a key part of establishing social capital.

In Jordan, the criticisms of the public education system are similar to so many other places in the world: learning based on memorisation; inappropriate curricula taught formally to big classes; low levels of critical thinking. Middle-class Jordanians send their children to private schools where they can study the International Baccalaureate, undertake project-based learning and enjoy far higher levels of interactivity. A university degree is absolutely no guarantee of employment – according to an IMF report the unemployment rate amongst graduates is 15 percent. [32] Again, the key has to be engaging the private sector fully in the enterprise because many businesses in Jordan do not trust the accreditation of schools or universities. JCEF does this through targeting CEOs (often leveraging the contacts of its Board) and through the Human Resources Society. Public education is changing – but slowly.

Mayyada Abu Jaber believes that JCEF has established proof of concept, and embodies the prototype. She points to the endorsement that JCEF's model has received from the IMF's May 2012 report on Jordan.

'Why can't this be scaled up? We reach only 1000 students a year. It could easily be 10,000. Of course we have to maintain quality, but we know how to do that too. We have strong systems of monitoring and evaluation: we do pre- and post-test evaluation in the workplace and with employers; we do focus groups; we evaluate our trainers; and we've got good MIS systems. There is no reason why this can't be extended across the whole country. Business is ready.'

There is an urgent need for similar interventions in many advanced industrialised economies too. Based in San Francisco, California, Growth Sector is the brainchild of Dave Gruber who has many years' experience in workforce development in the USA. It is a not-for-profit workforce intermediary with an equity mission, similar to JCEF. But it is subtly different – its role is to kick-start the reform of the existing public education system rather than bypass it.

The reason for this is Gruber's insight that people failed by the schooling system in the US will not gain access to high-paying jobs through job- or skill-specific short-term programmes. In an economy that rewards education and skills, it is increasingly a myth to believe that if you start out with entry-level jobs you can work your way up, especially in the high growth sectors of engineering and technology.

Therefore, in the Californian context, where there is near-universal access to the community college system, it does not make sense to construct a separate system for workforce development. Rather, through redesigning community colleges in partnership with employers (with the offer of jobs at the end), viable and successful pathways could be created.

The reform is desperately needed. Community College enrolment in the US is at a recession-fuelled all-time high. [33] Yet in places like Chicago, for instance, graduation is an appalling 10 percent, which has led Mayor Rahm Emanuel to take decisive action to reorganise the system. [34] Chicago has an unemployment rate of around 10 percent and yet there are 100,000 job vacancies because not enough people are trained. US Undersecretary of Education Martha Kanter does not mince her words when discussing the sector: 'The assessment system is broken, and the curriculum out of date. Remediation is in the 18th century.'

Hence Growth Sector and similar initiatives across the US, such as Year Up, are partnering with community colleges to re-fashion their pedagogy and curricula towards authentic learning. This means more project-based, personalised and collaborative learning – the features that leaders like Omnia are modelling.

Even in countries lacking the most basic infrastructure, the same principles of learning apply. Where schools, training centres and community colleges do not exist, the vehicle for learning is often technology. In many parts of Africa, where internet connection is not yet widely available, innovators are using what there is – in the case of the following case study, radio. Deploying the most appropriate technology currently available, innovators are providing the means to match the needed skills in the right places to the right people.

DEPLOYING AVAILABLE TECHNOLOGY IN RURAL NIGERIA

In 2003, aged 21, Nnaemeka Ikegwonu started Smallholder Farmers Rural Radio 'in his mind'. Nnaemeka comes from oil-rich Imo State in south-west Nigeria. A local man with a passion for journalism and agriculture, he was struck by the wasted effort of poor, underperforming farmers in the rural areas he visited. His vision was for a local radio station with the capacity to reach all farmers in Imo State through their small, ubiquitous, transistor radios. It would share information on farming techniques, market prices, weather, opportunities for small government loans, where to get the best seed – and would radically improve their yield and livelihoods as a result. In the early days, he worked to raise funds and test the idea with local people. He distributed high quality seed to demonstrate his good intent and his knowledge and to build trust with farmers. In 2007, UNESCO provided funding to start the radio station proper. Having laid the groundwork with local people, it was an instant hit and quickly reached millions.

The radio station was originally very strict about its agricultural remit – the programmes focused purely on farming techniques, tips, insights and information about local markets. They were delivered by the central Smallholder Farmers Rural Radio team. Today, local broadcasters, speaking in the many Ibo dialects, have been trained to deliver the programmes: 'It gives it more passion and creates a bond with listeners,' says Nnaemeka. As the broadcasters in the remote village of Obitti

explain, they wrap the content in folk stories and music so that people are entertained while they learn how to get the best results from their crops. The broadcasters do this in their spare time. During the day, they make money as drivers, teachers and engineers. From 7:00 pm onwards, they talk to local smallholders about the best planting distance for maize (25 centimetres) or rice (75 centimetres). They work in a concrete hut with a corrugated iron roof, equipped with a computer and a big, red microphone. A loud, diesel generator provides power for their work – and lots of fumes. They laugh when asked whether they enjoy it: 'Of course!... (we are) bringing people out of the darkness.'

The local farmers of Obitti are just as enthusiastic. 'Life is sweet now,' says Orioha, her thin, crinkled face wreathed in smiles. 'Yield has increased (in everything) – maize, yam, cassava, okra, melon, peppers, groundnuts.' The radio station's own evaluation confirms this. The team inspects the fields in areas where they are working and has seen improved practices, product quality and yield. The knock on effect is that local markets are bustling, says Nnaemeka: 'More buyers now come… they know they will find cheap, good quality products.'

Ugochukwu Igbokwe, the radio station's manager, stresses that they have learnt that the impact on farmers' whole lives – not just on their agricultural techniques – is critically important: 'Health is wealth for these farmers. Many of them keep labouring without enough sleep or nutrition. They cycle long distances to work and often have bad hygiene at home. They get sick, have high blood pressure and we hear stories of farmers dying of heart attacks by the side of the road.' So it has become an urgent priority for the station to run programmes on health and hygiene alongside harvesting and cultivation. Most programmes are repeated several times – important for farmers whose time is at a premium.

'Listening groups' help to embed the learning. Local farmers meet regularly to catch new programmes, many people like coming together to listen. There are lots of good reasons for this. For a start, most smallholders are members of a local cooperative, helping each other to raise crops and working together to transport and sell them. Improving collective productivity is in everyone's interest. Listening groups also allow farmers to ask each other questions, discuss what they have heard, and hold each other to account for really using new techniques. And it is fun.

Listening groups convey information both to and from the radio station. Members share their new knowledge with farmers in and beyond the village who do not receive the programmes. They also constantly inform Ugochukwu and the broadcasters about what is useful and what is not – like reducing the programme length from 30 to 10 minutes to fit in better with their busy lives.

Over time, the success of the radio station has 'made it obvious' that complementary programmes are necessary to improve the quality of farmers' lives. One of these is a small-scale micro finance programme. The value of the learning could not be realised without small loans to help farmers put it into practice. Sometimes, this is as simple as investing in tools and labour to help clear bigger areas of land to work at scale. So far, all loans have been repaid through higher yield and profit.

Future Farmers is another 'obvious' extension of their work. It began when young people started coming to the radio station to ask for money. When the team asked why it found that the young people were working hard for their parents, but did not get paid themselves. So instead of paying money, the team set up a programme that would enable young people to work for themselves, learn techniques to help them build a better future, and make money at the same time. 'It is about catching them young,' says Emeka Lewechi who leads the Future Farmers programme. 'It is about (them) becoming creators of jobs, not seekers.'

Future Farmers works with young people in secondary schools. It trains them in modern agricultural techniques and helps them to set up smallholdings on school premises. At Isu Girls Secondary School, the young women chose to start a poultry farm. The profits go to repay Future Farmers for their investment, grow the farm, and are also given as small loans to young women to start their own farms at home. Future Farmers stresses that young people are learning about business as well as farming. They have to understand profit, marketing and business planning to make the programme work.

Young people make up half of Africa's population. Today, millions more young Africans complete primary school than was the case a decade ago; yet their subsequent options remain limited. Accelerating the use of technologies – old and new – must be a part of the solution. One rapid growth area has been the acquisition of skills online. Whether it is the Khan Academy, or MIT and Harvard's OpenCourseWare, these innovations represent serious alternatives to the institutional delivery model.

Africa's one billion people use only 4 percent of the world's electricity [35] and many cannot afford to charge a computer, let alone buy one. However, half the population now owns a mobile phone. [36] This has led phone users and developers to be more resourceful, and mobiles are being used in Africa to do things that advanced economies are only now beginning to pick up on – from transferring money to sharing market prices for grain. What is missing is the pedagogy and the content to be deployed through this medium. Innovators such as InnoOmnia in Finland are rapidly evolving the practice of m-learning. Finland's

teachers and Nigeria's farmers may be converging on some shared solutions, through the contextualised exploitation of technology to update and match skills rapidly and effectively.

This convergence is true for all the major learning principles that emerge from this chapter. Skills acquisition in India, Jordan, USA, Nigeria and Finland may look very different on the surface, but there are seven key lessons that they agree on:

1. Start with demand: build the deep connections with employers (including the self-employed, as in Africa) that allow learning to be relevant, high quality and up to date

2. Keep looking forward – always think about what's coming next

3. Ensure that learning is grounded in and connected with real life

4. Integrate 'vocational learning' with mainstream education and 'academic' learning

5. Design learning to be flexible and personalised to the highest degree possible

6. Build in substantial and essential collaborative experiences

7. Exploit to the maximum every technology available

This chapter has focused on how innovators are seeking to match and update the skills and knowledge that people around the world need to flourish, and which fast-changing economies require. But as 2iE showed in Chapter 2, simply to achieve the more efficient acquisition of skills and knowledge is not enough to be truly transformational. Learning how to deploy them to tackle the complex challenges that characterise today's world is also imperative. Chapter 4 looks at how innovators from Brazil to China are enabling people to deal with such complex problems and generate solutions to them.

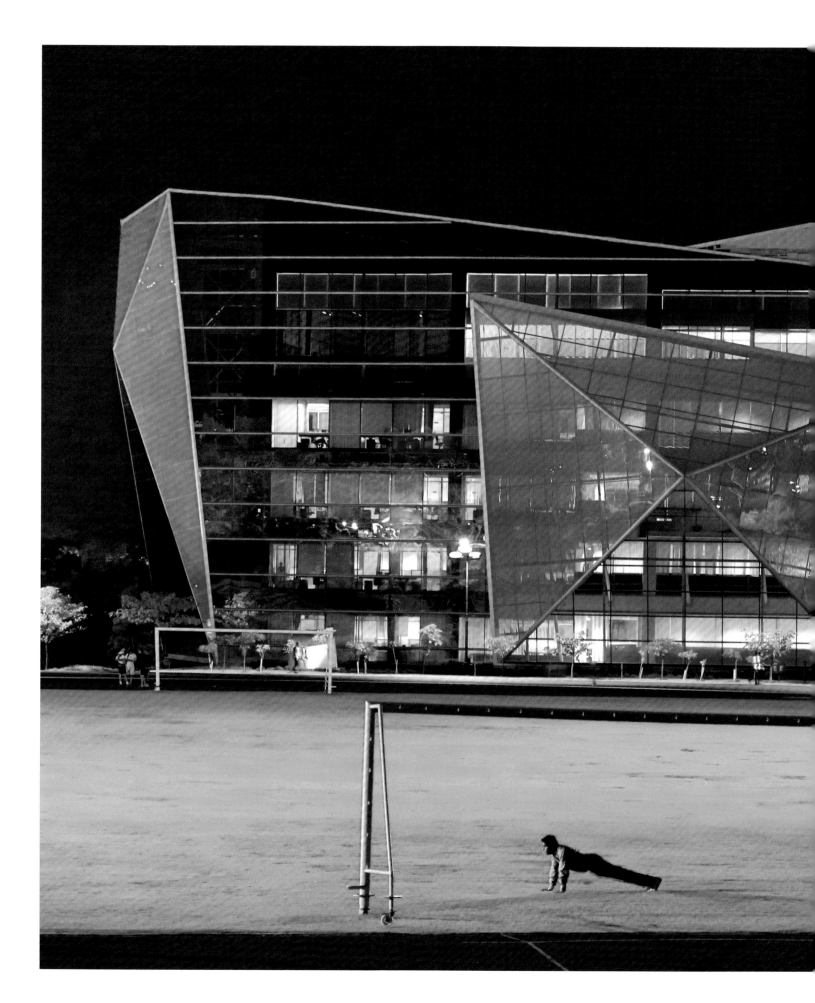

The leisure and sporting
facilities at Infosys, Mysore,
overlooked by the company
offices.

Two of the 20,000 trainees
at Infosys' Global Education
Centre (GEC) in Mysore.

Students designing a swing
at Lumiar school, São Paolo.

CHAPTER 4

THE BIGGER PICTURE

Generating solutions

We always treat problems as a good thing here at Lumiar. Problems require solutions, and it's in finding the solutions that the learning happens … We teach our students that there's no such thing as failure. We encourage them to think: Well, that didn't work. So why didn't it work? Now let's try again.

Joanna Gayotto
Headmistress, Lumiar school, São Paolo

Florence Tobo Lobe is suffused with energy as she tells the story of the Rubisadt Foundation. It is a story that begins with her own upbringing in Cameroon – an 'easy' childhood with parents who were determined to buck the trend and give their daughter the best possible education. The young Florence flourished, ending up as a senior lecturer in chemistry in Paris.

Demanding and interesting as her job in France was, however, she knew she wanted to return to Cameroon to contribute to the place she came from. There, many young people were used to learning by rote, without understanding what their knowledge really meant. Classes were detached from the challenges of real life in Cameroon and girls were heavily outnumbered by boys.

Florence began by working with young people of both sexes at secondary school to try and improve the nature of learning and the quality of science expertise. Quickly, she became determined that this work should focus on young women. The reasons were manifold. Firstly, she was horrified at the waste of talent and potential. She saw that young women were doing well at primary school – better than boys – but began dropping out during secondary school when the financial and social pressures became too great. At the same time, driving around Cameroon's cities, she noticed the shocking number of women – many younger than those she worked with at secondary school – out on the streets, 'selling their charms'. She later found that many were attracted to prostitution by older women in their trade being driven around in smart cars, with expensive clothes. They were aspirational role models.

The Rubisadt Foundation offers supplementary science classes and summer camps to talented African high school girls. Its curriculum is shaped from two directions – the scientific content and the personal development that Florence believes is required to enable students to make the most of what they learn. The 'building personality' content is totally bespoke. It all starts with a one-on-one conversation between Florence (or, today, one of her staff) and a young woman: Who are you? What do you enjoy? How do you see your future? She then insists on a variety of other interviews to understand fully the young woman's environment – individual conversations with her mother, then her father (if she has one), and her favourite teacher, and group conversations with both parents and with her whole family.

These activities are critical to developing the 'personality' that Florence believes is required to be a voracious learner and to go on and contribute to your country. In a complex world in which individuals often find themselves confronted by adversity and societies face complicated challenges, it is not enough to acquire knowledge and skills. The girls in Cameroon thrived at primary school, but as they got older they did not have the resilience or independence to resist the negative influences and

pressures of their environment. To develop these capabilities they needed support and positive role models. It is this which turns Rubistadt's supplementary classes into something much more than additional tuition; they are giving students a whole new world view, self-awareness and sense of responsibility both for themselves and their communities.

The Rubisadt Foundation's work, however, does not stop at personal development – it is also seeking to develop a generation of top scientists. Florence wanted to ensure that students would go on to make Cameroon's economy more healthy and competitive, and to be able to apply their science knowledge to some of Africa's most pressing issues, such as water, sanitation and public health. This demands not only expertise in science, but also high-level cognitive abilities such as creativity, collaboration and critical thinking – what are often called problem-solving abilities or '21st-century skills'.

The innovations explored in this chapter offer further examples of the ways in which different innovative learning models are generating solutions at the complex intersection between individual, national and global needs.

THE RISING SUN ENERGY CENTER: BUILDING RESILIENCE, ADAPTABILITY AND PURPOSE

The Rising Sun Energy Center began as a grassroots initiative in Santa Cruz, California, in 1994, before moving to Berkeley in 2000. It is now a thriving non-profit operating across the San Francisco Bay Area, offering green workforce development and employment opportunities to young people and adults. Promoting energy efficiency is one of its principal aims. So too is the empowerment of marginalised groups and the reduction of unemployment. Such a multi-faceted approach is a response to what can be described as a classically complex 21st-century problem.

According to the World Wildlife Fund (WWF), unsustainable consumption patterns make humanity's environmental footprint 31 times larger than the planet's capacity to produce these resources. [37] Rising Sun attempts to address the issue of sustainability at the same time as the issue of employment, by upskilling and mobilising young people and adults to work in the green economy. Over the last ten years the team have refined their approach to make it as successful as possible at transforming the lives of those they work with. Take an imaginary person – we'll call him Robert – who has grown up in a deprived part of Richmond near San Francisco, ranked by the FBI as one of the top 20 most dangerous cities in the USA. Gang activity in Richmond is rife: more often than not, if you live in the north of the area it is

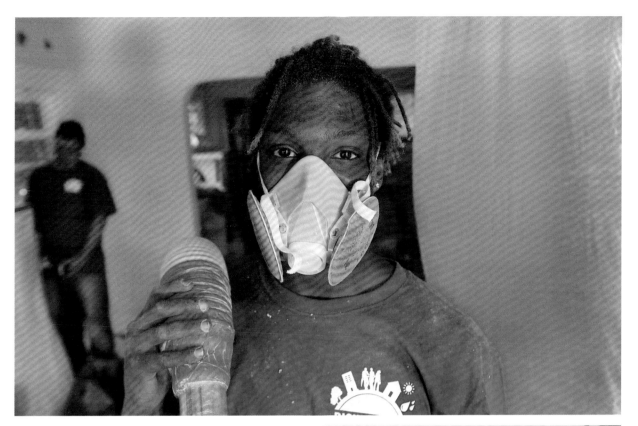

One of Rising Sun's young energy specialists preparing to insulate a low-income home in Berkeley, California. Since the year 2000, Rising Sun has serviced wover 16,000 homes.

Sophie Barich and Tafari Maynard, energy specialists on the CYES programme, inspecting work carried out in Marin County, California.

Every summer, Rising
Sun's California Youth Energy
Services (CYES) trains
up almost 100 young people
from 10 cities in California.
Many come from difficult
backgrounds.

dangerous to venture into the south, and vice versa. Robert has three brothers, two of whom are heavily involved in gangs. The third brother is in prison for drug dealing. Having dropped out of school without any qualifications, Robert does not have many prospects. To add to this, he is African American, which means that he is at an even higher risk of unemployment than his caucasian friends; at the end of 2011, the unemployment rate for African Americans was 15.8 percent in the US – more than double that for caucasian people. [38] Robert lives with his aunt, who has recently told him that he is going to have to move out. He is worried about becoming homeless. Gang involvement looks increasingly inevitable. It is fair to assume that climate change is the last thing on Robert's mind.

Robert is a fictional character, but stories like his abound amongst the young people and adults who work for Rising Sun. Disadvantage is certainly not a prerequisite for involvement with the organisation, but a substantial number of the young people come from difficult backgrounds: some have children, some have criminal records, many have few or no qualifications.

The first part of Rising Sun's challenge, then, is to equip these young people with the relevant skills to enable them to work in the local green economy – this is the kind of 'skills matching' discussed in Chapter 3. Many of these skills are fairly routine and manual, such as the ability to change light bulbs and adjust the water flow in homeowners' taps. The other – considerably more complex – part of the challenge is to find a way to help young people like Robert to resist the potentially negative influences of their environment. Rising Sun also encourages them to engage with the wider problem of climate change, and motivates them to build brighter futures for themselves and their communities to ensure that the impact of the organisation is long-term and sustainable. As Executive Director Jodi Pincus puts it, 'We are teaching these young people how to be leaders, experts, specialists, educators, and future civic citizens.' And all this must be done within a financially robust business model.

Rising Sun makes it look easy. 'We call it the triple win strategy,' says Jodi, referring to the organisation's best-established programme, the California Youth Energy Services (CYES). Every summer, CYES trains up almost 100 young people from 10 cities in California in house assessments and retrofitting skills so that they can deliver free 'green house calls' to residents in the San Francisco Bay Area. The 'sell' to residents is that they can reduce their energy bills for free. How? Because the Cities fund 20 percent of the programme out of a desire to meet their greenhouse gas reduction targets and to promote local youth employment. The rest of the funding comes from the energy company PG&E, which is mandated to reduce energy consumption. So everybody wins. Since the year 2000, Rising Sun has retro-fitted over 16,000 homes, worked with

over 1000 young people and reduced over 60,000 metric tons of CO_2 greenhouse gas emissions. How do they do it?

Effective collaboration is a central pillar of the organisation. The Rising Sun team is made up of a mix of people, each with different capabilities, interests and motivations. Some are more interested in workforce development, while for others this is just 'the icing on the cake' – tackling climate change is the most essential aspect of what Rising Sun does. This diversity is regarded as one of the organisation's key strengths. As one employee puts it, 'We balance each other out.' Staff members are encouraged to see themselves as being arranged around the points of a compass according to their unique leadership qualities: those in the 'north' provide direction; those in the east are the visionaries; those in the south are in touch with their emotions; and those in the west are the 'implementers'. Together, they form a well-rounded, complementary team with the capacity to tackle problems from different angles. 'I'm definitely an implementer,' says Heather Hochrein, Head of the CYES programme. 'But Jodi is a visionary. She can dream about how things can be.'

In addition to these permanent staff, Rising Sun's staff swells from around 20 to 130 during the summer months, in order to deliver the CYES programme. This way of working might be held up as an early example of 'swarming', where teams of people who know little about one another come together to solve a particular problem, before quickly dispersing again. In a study of what the world of work will look like in ten years, the global research organisation Gartner predicts that swarming will become increasingly characteristic of the way in which workers organise themselves. [39] The sharp increase in the numbers of people on Rising Sun's payroll presents a huge logistical challenge, but also strengthens the programme. Included in the temporary staff are site managers and assistant managers, who are recruited to help train, supervise and coach each CYES team (ten in total – one for each city). They come from a variety of backgrounds – many are university students or recent graduates – bringing passion, purpose and energy to the job, and ensuring that the organisation benefits from a regular flow of new ideas and perspectives.

Mentoring and coaching is an integral part of Rising Sun's work – in order to contribute effectively, young people need to feel confident and supported. Adrian Sacharski is the 25-year-old manager of the CYES Richmond team and Rising Sun's full-time Community Outreach Manager. Impressively articulate and passionate, he confesses to having been a 'tearaway' when he was younger: he dropped out of high school in San Francisco and holds a criminal record for doing 'some stupid things' in his teenage years. He is driven by the desire to offer better opportunities to young people. 'I feel really strongly about making a connection with these youth. There's not enough out there to support them in the transitional phase of life, when they're just figuring out what they want to do. It's easy to get lost in the system, to fall into the wrong crowds… With my background, I get where they're coming from – and I try my best to be a good role model to them.'

With this nurturing infrastructure in place, Rising Sun can focus on building resilience and responsibility. The 'youth employment training model' that Rising Sun has developed over the years posits resilience as the core skill that young people need to succeed in work and life. The training includes role plays and scenarios that encourage young people to develop resilience as well as key soft skills such as conflict resolution, communication skills and decision-making: 'One of your friends is an exemplary team member but has recently been showing up late for work and seems to be upset about something. What do you do?' 'A homeowner starts shouting that you have broken his expensive vase and demanding that you pay for it, but you know that you did not touch the vase and you are fairly certain that you noticed that it was already broken. What do you do?' CYES members work through these problems together through discussion and debate. When the work starts, however, they will not have recourse to this kind of structured activity. This is where they can really put their independence of thought and critical-thinking skills into practice.

The independence given to these youth is crucial in supporting them to take responsibility. After a week of intensive training, they venture in pairs to do marketing and outreach for the programme, or to retrofit people's homes. Supervision and monitoring is kept to a minimum, forcing the young people to think on their feet. The majority of them rise to the challenge. 'Rising Sun don't tell you what to do – they trust you to work it out for yourself,' says one 15-year-old, who has been expelled from several schools in the San Francisco Bay Area. He is, according to his site manager, one of the best young energy specialists on the programme: 'smart, professional, charismatic, and an excellent communicator.' Each summer, feedback from homeowners routinely reflects the outstanding levels of service, with 90 percent of green house calls being rated 'very good' or 'excellent'. Residents often report 'astonishment' at the maturity of the young people who come into their homes.

One common challenge that the young people face is suspicion from homeowners: 'Sometimes based on the fact that they're young, sometimes based on racial stereotypes. People are expecting them to do something amiss.' Fifteen-year-old Rodell, an African–American young man from Richmond, has occasionally encountered such prejudices: 'You can see it in their eyes… when you come into their homes, they're on edge.' Over time he has learnt how to deal with it. 'Knowing what you're doing is one thing. For sure, you have to know what you're talking about. But that's not enough. It's all in the body language too. You walk in: back straight, smiling. Be polite – offer to take your shoes off. Eye contact is important. You have to be friendly and attentive, but also brisk and professional – show them that you're here to do a job, and to do it well. Win their trust.' He shrugs. 'In the end, it's easy. You just have to prove them wrong.' In these kinds of scenarios, the CYES members learn an important lesson: having knowledge and skills is a vital foundational step in being able to do a job well, but dealing with new and unexpected problems as they arise requires more abstract problem-solving abilities such as ingenuity and interpersonal skills.

To become truly adaptable, learners also need to understand where their skills and knowledge fit into a bigger picture, so they can flexibly apply what they know elsewhere. At Rising Sun, educating young people how to do energy upgrades of people's homes is only one small part of the task at hand; they must also be given a comprehensive sense of why this kind of work is necessary, and be motivated to *care*. Each summer programme begins and ends with a celebratory event, which brings all of the CYES teams together. According to Jodi, 'It helps them to feel part of something important, bigger than themselves – to inspire them.'

In addition, a large proportion of the training is devoted to teaching the youth about the effects of climate change. This is important, because it prepares them for the final part of the green house calls, which involves 'educating' residents about why and how they can adopt other sustainable behaviours and technologies – thus serving as ambassadors for more sustainable living. 'Did you know that it's better to water your garden in the morning rather than the evening, because it's cooler?' 'Ever considered increasing the insulation in your attic?' Most of the young people on the programme are proud to be seen as 'educators' and 'experts' doing something of benefit for their communities and the wider world. Many put what they have learnt into practice in other areas of their lives. 'I have to admit that I still take long showers,' laughs 19-year-old Delonda, member of the Richmond CYES team. 'But I try to practice what I preach. Before I joined Rising Sun I didn't know anything about global warming. Now, when I go to friends' houses I tell them "Turn that TV off – don't you know it's damaging our planet?!"'

This is Delonda's third summer working for CYES – those who do well are always given the opportunity to return. She is now enrolled in a college course, studying TV and radio broadcasting. Seventy percent of the Richmond youth who do CYES end up either in a job or back in education. With pastoral and practical support from Rising Sun and the hands-on experience of training and working 'in the field', young people become true 21st-century problem-solvers, not just focused on retrofitting houses, but preoccupied by questions such as: How can I use what I have learnt to persuade my friends and family to care about climate change? How can I use what I have learnt to change my own life? How can I use what I have learnt to build a better future – for myself and the world?

But Rising Sun must remain agile. Already there are signs that the energy upgrade business will soon be a thing of the past. Homeowners are becoming more environmentally conscious and domestic fittings are now made to be more energy efficient. Jodi and her team are not complacent. An ideas board in their Berkeley office is crammed with ideas for how to take the organisation forward – composting and environmentally-friendly lawn-landscaping are amongst the suggestions. In recent years, Rising Sun has also diversified, developing a successful Green Energy Training Services (GETS) programme for adults facing barriers to employment. This is designed to give learners a Building Performance Institute-approved certification that prepares them for entry-level jobs in the green construction industry. In addition, Rising Sun runs a small social enterprise – graduates of GETS gain on-the-job training and employment in energy efficiency work alongside soft skills training that supports them to progress to long-term green careers. It has also identified an opportunity to partner with the Lawrence Berkeley National Laboratory on the Department of Energy's Appliance Standards Programme. 'They want to meter energy usage of 1000 common use appliances in people's homes,' explains Jodi. 'And we figured, if we're already sending our youth into all these homes, why not team up with them and help them perform this world class study?' Leveraging resources through mutually beneficial partnerships has always been an important feature of Rising Sun's work.

Rising Sun is impressive on every level. Dynamic and innovative, the team are modeling how to respond to a complex world at the same time as equipping young people and adults with resilience, adaptability, self-awareness, collaboration, ingenuity and purpose. Most of all, they are transforming lives, and in many cases doing so where formal education systems have failed.

———

Rising Sun is an example of an organisation that generates 'blended value – what results when businesses, whether for-profit or non-profit, create value in multiple dimensions – economic, social or environmental.' [40] In his most recent book *The Zeronauts: Breaking the Sustainability Barrier*, John Elkington – a leading thinker on corporate social responsibility and Founding Partner and Executive Chairman of Volans, a future-focused business working at the intersection of the sustainability, innovation and entrepreneurship movements – looks at those 'pioneers' who are developing innovative solutions to the sustainability challenge. He believes that these 'entrepreneurs, innovators and investors' are part of a general trend that is driving businesses towards a more sustainable future. Faced with a world in which climate change, food security issues and gas and oil shortages threaten their own survival, businesses are increasingly taking the lead in responding to some of the world's most pressing problems.

Formal educational spheres are more slow-moving, often treating the world, in Elkington's words, as a 'controlled experiment in which all of the variables are fixed and known'. Yet some innovations in formal education, like SUSTC in China, are beginning to address this lack of urgency. Educational reform has been on the cards in China for some time. As international scholar, author and speaker Professor Yong Zhao notes, 'Recognising the negative consequences of "test-oriented education", China has launched a series of national reforms to cultivate more creative citizens.' This is because, while parts of China perform highly in international assessments, many believe that the country's failure to develop innovative talents threatens to undermine its competitive edge. In 2008, merely 473 innovations from China were recognised by the world's leading patent offices outside China in 2008 compared with 14,399 from the USA. Additionally, some observers point to the fact that the education system ignores the importance of developing 'intangible qualities such as initiative, attitude, and morals'. [41] In one part of China, however, SUSTC is proving that radical change is possible, and laying the foundations for a new generation of innovative problem-solvers.

SUSTC: INNOVATING FOR THE FUTURE

———

Seen from above, Shenzhen glitters. Thirty years ago it was nothing more than a tiny fishing village set amongst forested hills and mango trees. But due to its proximity to Hong Kong it was singled out in 1979 as China's first 'free economic zone', spearheading China's experiments with a more open market economy. With 14 million people now living and working amidst its towering skyscrapers, today the area stands as a powerful symbol of the success of that experiment.

Recently, however, the local economy – as in the rest of China – has been slowing. Keen to replace a struggling manufacturing-based economy with a knowledge-intensive one, the Shenzhen authorities recognised that, for this kind of transition to be successfully achieved, it was necessary to create an international, cutting-edge R&D university. They envisioned that this university would lead innovation within China's higher education system, collaborating with the wider world in a quest to generate knowledge that could meet local, national and international needs. In March 2011, SUSTC admitted its first class of 45 undergraduate students.

With proposed academic programmes in Environmental Preservation, New Energies, Financial Mathematics, Future Cities and Nanotechnology, SUSTC seeks to offer the highest quality teaching and research on some of society's most topical issues, while also aiming to play a prominent role in educating young people to be 'free thinkers'. 'Of course our students must, first and foremost, have solid foundational and academic knowledge,' says Deputy Director Dr Han Wei. 'But we also want them to have a global perspective, to be able to think independently, rationally and critically, and to have a positive view about life and a sense of agency.'

The person appointed to be the President of SUSTC was Professor Qingshi Zhu, a respected scholar and former president of the University of Science and Technology of China, who is known for speaking out against senseless bureaucracy – something that, in his view, only serves to compromise the quality of education in China. As he sees it, it is essential to have the right conditions in place to be able to develop true problem-solvers: to give them the space, support and freedom to think critically, be creative, and communicate and collaborate in effective ways. 'University is an academic organisation,' Professor Zhu points out. 'Unless it has autonomy to manage its own institutional affairs, it will not be able to truly pursue academic excellence or achieve high quality within its core functions.'

Building an environment conducive to innovation includes, for SUSTC, being able to achieve an unprecedented level of independence from political interference. In one radical move, SUSTC has started to establish a collaborative university council formed, in equal parts, of university and government representatives as well as representatives from the broader society such as businessmen and other highly reputable professionals. Students will also be involved in key decisions where relevant.

Reforming the way in which skills and capabilities are assessed has also been one of SUSTC's projects. This problem will be a familiar one to educators across the world: education systems are still in thrall to old-fashioned assessment methods that do not adequately reflect the importance of '21st-century skills' such as problem-solving. In China's case, the notorious *Gao Kao* is a gruelling set of national college entrance exams that are widely criticised as being little more than a memorisation test. 'Because of the test,' says Minghao He, a student at SUSTC, 'high school teachers put all of their efforts into helping students to pass the college entrance exam rather than improving the quality of their knowledge. The priority is wrong – we need to learn new and important skills, not how to regurgitate information.' Last year, in order to rush the first intake of students through its doors, the university did not have time to administer the *Gao Kao*, a move which was both highly controversial and widely applauded.

Future intakes of students at SUSTC will have to take the *Gao Kao*: not taking it could jeopardise their futures. However, the university has reached an agreement with the Ministry of Education to administer a supplementary test of its own in order to reflect the fact that it is not simply looking for those students who can get the highest test marks. Certainly, the ability to retain knowledge and information is important, but SUSTC's test also includes sections to assess students' powers of concentration, imagination and perception. 'In one question, for example,' explains President Zhu, 'we might give students a pen. And we might ask, "How many uses can you think of for this pen?" It's a simple question, but some students can think of five or six different uses, and others can think of thirty. We're looking for those individuals with imagination.'

SUSTC's fight for autonomy and the right to innovate has sparked controversy across China and made it the subject of much media interest. The Ministry of Education has given the university a 'three-year preparation time' and continues to monitor SUSTC's progress closely. But despite numerous obstacles, there are several enabling factors in place that could aid the university's ultimate success: it has the backing (and the funding) of the Shenzhen authorities, who have a long history of supporting innovation and conducting reform; it was able to attract experienced faculty members, many of whom had worked for long periods abroad and who brought with them a wealth of expertise and insights; and it was led and supported by people who had the personal confidence and conviction that there was a real need for this kind of innovation. Professor David Shuk-yin Tong had almost reached retirement when he met with his 'good friend' Professor Zhu. 'He said to me, there's a lot of work to be done here – can you help?' He smiles wryly. 'I couldn't resist the opportunity to be part of building something new for China. There's a great spirit here. A spirit of "Why not? Why can't we do things better?"'

Although the university is still at an early stage of development, the learning design at SUSTC has a number of innovative features. Teaching is interdisciplinary, with departments working together to offer cross-disciplinary modules that enable students to apply their knowledge across subject boundaries. There is also an emphasis on enquiry and challenge, with students encouraged at all times to ask questions, discuss and debate. Collaboration and teamwork is also a highly valued skill, as is the application of knowledge to real-world issues. One professor recently entered two groups of students into MIT's International Genetically Engineered Machine (iGEM) competition, where teams of students from all over the world compete to develop new biological systems. Another young professor recently organised the students into eight teams, all dedicated to developing a product that could be put to use in the real world. One group, for example, developed a walking aid that was activated by light. 'The students had to come up with the ideas themselves, by working together,' says Professor Hongyu Yu. 'They had to bring their creativity to what they had learnt.' The project ended with a final competition in which the products were ranked and students were given the opportunity to challenge one another's designs.

Relaxation and exercise
at SUSTC, Shenzhen.
The University aims to develop
a generation of independent
thinkers and problem-solvers,
and to grow into a campus
of 8000 students.

SUSTC is working hard to develop a generation of young people who are independent thinkers and problem-solvers, and has ambitions to grow from a small campus of 45 students into one of 8000, with a postgraduate as well as undergraduate facility. It will not be easy to achieve these goals, but staff are optimistic: 'I have high hopes,' says Professor Tong. 'We don't know what the future will look like, but I think good things will come of SUSTC. Unexpected things.'

Professor Tong's final comment reveals an important point – we do not yet know what the future holds. The best that educators can do is to develop students who not only have foundational knowledge and skills, but who are also passionate about learning and who are engaged with the world, so that when problems do arise they have the motivation as well as the ability to apply what they know. Indeed, based on a fifteen-year study on what constitutes 'good work', Professor Howard Gardner, an American developmental psychologist best known for his theory of 'multiple intelligences', identifies engagement – along with excellence and ethics – as one of the three most important principles.

Unfortunately, education systems around the world are failing, at a very basic level, to engage students in learning. This is reflected in high dropout rates and high levels of disengagement for those who remain in school. In Brazil, school attendance rates for 5-14 year olds have increased from 25 percent in 1940 to 97 percent today, but apathy still characterises the attitude of many students and teachers within the public education system. Reflecting on his experiences at a school in São Paolo, one recent graduate says, 'I was always frustrated with the fact that there was not enough discovery – not enough finding out for yourself. Things were presented to you as if knowledge was a closed box, abstract and detached from the real world.'

São Paolo – the largest city in the southern hemisphere – is feeling the strain of an inadequate education system. 'São Paolo is crazy,' says one disgruntled local. 'We pay almost 40 percent in taxes, and what do we get for it? Roads choked with traffic day and night. Health care that we have to pay for. Security issues. And a government which can't seem to find a solution to any of these problems.' It is not just the public who want more from their leaders. Some of São Paolo's top businesses frequently advertise their senior positions for eight or nine months at a time, without finding a suitable candidate to fill the post. The high-level cognitive abilities required, from critical thinking and ingenuity to flexibility and collaboration, can be hard to find. The Brazilian government has begun a new set of programmes around innovation in education; but business has taken the initiative too.

One businessman who recognised education's shortfalls is Ricardo Semler, self-described maverick and former CEO of the Brazilian company SEMCO. In 2003, Semler published *The Seven Day Weekend*. This best-selling book makes the case for a highly unorthodox approach to management that involves giving staff more autonomy rather than enforcing rigid corporate rules and hierarchies. Under Semler's leadership, SEMCO flourished, with gross revenues increasing from $4 million in 1984 to $65 million in 2004. But Semler saw that the public schools in Brazil were lagging behind in developing ways to unleash young people's problem-solving abilities and creative talents, so he turned his attention to education. In 2002, the first Lumiar school was born. There are now three in existence – two private and one public, all in the state of São Paulo. The final part of this chapter will be devoted to exploring some of the learning principles on which Lumiar is founded, and the techniques that can be used to provide an education focused on developing problem-solving abilities – as well as true engagement.

THE CASE OF LUMIAR: ENGAGING MINDS, SOLVING PROBLEMS

LEARN TO CHALLENGE AND QUESTION

It's Wednesday afternoon, the remains of lunch have been cleared away and the students at Lumiar São Paolo – a kindergarten and primary school for children less than a year old up to age 14, based in the centre of São Paolo – have gathered together in preparation for a weekly ritual: the Circle. A cornerstone of the school's democratic philosophy, the Circle is an opportunity for all students and staff to discuss issues affecting the school and to vote on key decisions. All of those aged four and above must participate. They learn how to debate, how to express their opinions and how to value one another's contribution. The little ones don't always 'get it' – 'I had rice for dinner!' comes from one enthusiastic four-year-old. But the older students are patient: they remember what it was like to be that four-year-old, bewildered but eager.

One of the main points up for discussion this afternoon is the fact that a tea set was found smashed in the school kitchen. The culprits – a teenage boy and girl – admit to the mistake almost immediately: they were running, one of their coats caught the tea set, and it smashed. Mistakes of this kind are not punished in this school; instead, solutions are sought. In this particular case, a number of suggestions are put forward.

'We should pass rules which say that we can't run in school!' one student pipes up. The meeting co-ordinator, eight-year-old Paulo, writes this suggestion on the board. One of the tutors agrees: 'Students need to be more respectful of school property – they should be more cautious when playing in school.' These are useful lessons – but what to do about the missing tea set?

'Maybe we should divide the cost of the tea set between ourselves and the school can buy a new one.' This from one of 'the culprits', a slight blond-haired 13-year-old. A discussion ensues, in which the students and staff discuss whether or not it is fair for students to have to pay for school property.

At this point, six-year-old Bernardo interjects: 'You know, money isn't the answer to everything. If they simply give the school money to buy a new tea set, they might not learn from their actions. Their parents will give them the money and it will be too easy for them. How about the school gives them the money, and they have to do research themselves about where to buy a new tea set, and then go and buy it themselves from the shop in their own time? That will be more of a challenge – and it will teach them to be more careful next time.' There is a collective murmur. That was a good idea. That was a good solution to the problem.

The word that Talal Abu Ghazaleh, founder of a new online university, might use to characterise Bernardo's astonishingly mature contribution is 'wisdom'. According to Mr Abu Ghazaleh, in the 21st century, 'knowledge' is no longer enough – the future will be built by those who have the ability to apply insight and good judgement to different situations and challenges.

LEARN TO COLLABORATE

Collaboration is another key 21st-century skill. The curriculum at Lumiar is structured around projects that enable learning in multi-age teams. In the mornings the students can attend optional workshops, on unconventional topics that range from film-making to circus training. In the afternoons, groups of students work collaboratively with the staff to design projects that accord with their passions and interests. 'We discuss, agree, and then plan,' explains one member of staff. In order for the students to be able to collaborate effectively, it is vital that they learn to respect one another and make decisions as a group: learning with children who are older or younger than them is a good way to develop these skills and values. 'It's difficult for some of the older ones,' admits headmistress Joanna. 'But eventually they learn that everyone has something to contribute. Even the young ones make incredibly astute points. And it's great to see the reactions of the older students when that happens. You can see them thinking, "Wow. After all, maybe I'm not better than them. I just know different things, and think in different ways." That's an important lesson for them to learn – because after all, when they enter the real world, they won't be segregated by age, and they'll have to work and learn with and alongside all sorts of different people.'

ENGAGE WITH THE REAL WORLD

There are no teachers at Lumiar, but rather 'tutors' and 'masters' who work together to maximise the students' learning and support. While the tutors' task is to establish an emotional rapport with the students, liaise with their parents and monitor the students' progress, the masters are 'experts' drawn from the local community, who work part-time – generally for a period of about two months – to design and deliver projects that reflect their own expertise. This relationship enables the students to interact with adults who have knowledge and experience of the world beyond the educational sphere, thus making learning more authentic as masters bring their passions and experiences to bear on their teaching. The next step is for students to be able to apply their learning to real-world issues. This does not just have to take the form of sophisticated projects of the kind seen at SUSTC, but can also be as simple as encouraging students to bring in newspaper cuttings about topical issues and discussing them – an activity that is frequently practiced at Lumiar.

LEARN TO BE CREATIVE – SEE THE BIG PICTURE

Daniel Pink, author of several provocative books about the changing world of work, has called it 'symphony' – the ability to see the big picture, to sort out what really matters, and to see and integrate different things to create something new. In Pink's analysis, the future will be dominated by people who have mastered 'symphony', along with other creative abilities. [42] At Lumiar, multi-disciplinary learning helps students to develop creativity. Twenty-four-year-old Lucas is a master at the school; he has been working there on and off for two years, and studies Philosophy and Education at the University of São Paolo. He describes the organic form that projects at Lumiar frequently take:

> The students told me they wanted to destroy something. I thought, 'What can I do with this?' So we decided to learn about volcanoes – natural destruction. As part of the project we built a model of the local area. We visited buildings so that we could represent them in miniature, and learnt about their history. We then worked out how big a volcano would need to be in proportion to a town in order to destroy it completely. We learnt about the geography of volcanoes and about the reactions that take place inside them. And then came the time to destroy the model. By that point the students had worked hard and were sad to see the fruits of their labour demolished. So we were then able to explore some of the implications of destruction: moral, emotional, and economic. The students got what they had wanted – they had destroyed something – but in the process we delved into a vast array of other topics. And we learnt some important lessons along the way.

As learning wanders across subject boundaries, staff at Lumiar can ensure that students are progressing on the 'skill and competency matrix' that forms the backbone to education at Lumiar. According to this matrix, students must master a range of skills in different subject areas, such as numeracy and writing skills. They must also gain competencies, which include more abstract problem-solving abilities such as creativity.

Howard Gardner's work has played a major role in shaping thinking about creativity. His assertion is that creativity is a capability that cuts across skills and 'intelligences'. Before his theory of multiple intelligences, the basic assumption was that our brains were the equivalent of a single computer – either you had a really high functioning machine, a merely functional one, or a slightly slow one, and the power of the machine determined how well you would solve tasks and problems. Gardner's theory of multiple intelligences suggests that we have several different 'machines', including linguistic, mathematical, musical, spatial and kinaesthetic intelligences, and most of us will have some intelligences that are stronger than others. Yet when looking at indisputably great 'creatives' – from Einstein and Picasso to Stravinsky and Freud – Gardner finds that these people tend to have unusual combinations of two intelligences; that is, creativity arises when our different intelligences cross-fertilise one another. In order to fully realise our potential as creative individuals – and not just highly skilled experts in a field – 'cultivation and motivation' are for Gardner crucial conditions that enable our creativity to flourish. We must build environments that nurture the many different kinds of intelligences and encourage them to intersect and illuminate one another.

If creativity can be understood as the subconscious ability to make connections and associations between different ideas and experiences, learning at Lumiar strongly encourages this. It is complemented by the spatial layout of the school. The classrooms are not the uniform prison-like rectangles that are the familiar hallmarks of traditional schools. They might more accurately be described as a mismatched series of 'spaces' – long spaces, small spaces, rectangular spaces and square spaces – each colourfully decorated with the students' work. The notion that learning happens everywhere is strongly encouraged: teaching takes place outdoors, conversation flows around the dining table where students eat meals together, and 'play areas' are sites for exploration and enquiry. Students who find themselves disengaged for any reason are free to join other lessons elsewhere, or to learn by themselves. The priority of the school is to keep the students' curiosity alive and to ensure that they are really absorbed in their learning – what Howard Gardner might call 'creative flow'.

LEARN TO REFLECT

A final component of problem-solving is the capacity for reflection. Formative assessment methods at Lumiar build regular reflection into the learning process. For every project, students and staff have to set goals for themselves. At the end of every day they reflect on how well they have done, and redefine new goals for the next day. 'Our students do take the SARESP (the national test for primary school students in Brazil), and they do well at it,' says Joanna, 'but we see our own assessment methods as measuring the more important things, because they're tailored to individuals. Success after all for one student might be to get along better with others. For another, it might be to do better at maths. We need a more personalised system.'

Lucas sees the importance of self-reflection more holistically. 'São Paolo's a fast moving city,' he says. 'There aren't many opportunities for reflection. Everybody seems to be engaged in some kind of blind rat race, just working away. I think education's to blame in part. There's always someone choosing for us – defining what we learn, and what success looks like for us. I want to develop students who are more reflective, who have the ability to step back and say, "OK. But what is really important – for myself and the world in which I'm living?"'

While the innovative pedagogical approaches seen at Lumiar have thus far been applied in a relatively small set of schools, they have proved so successful that a coalition of international organisations – including Harvard's Project Zero, the University of Cambridge, the OECD and Microsoft – has recently assembled to explore the possibility of scaling them up across Brazil's broader public education system and in other parts of the world. This coalition – called Synapses – has already secured the go-ahead to test Lumiar's methodologies in ten public schools in Brazil. 'There's no "one size fits all" approach,' acknowledges Synapses's Director Ingrid Imenez, 'but we'll need to have certain key ingredients in place to make this work: didactic resources, technological enablers, workforce development strategy and strong evaluation processes.' Synapses's ultimate goal is to influence educational policy. 'These innovative learning opportunities must be for all,' says Ingrid. 'Above all, to really achieve systemic change, we'll need people to buy into our vision – to be inspired by it and committed to it.' Synapses's printed manifesto is a passionate call to action, demanding radical transformation of what it deems to be a hopelessly outdated education system. It opens with a memorable quote from Albert Einstein: 'No problem can be solved from the same consciousness that created it. We must learn to see the world anew.'

The seven principles outlined at the end of Chapter 3 are all relevant to learning that develops effective problem-solvers. What is different is emphasis. Real-world learning is even more important. So is personal development and the responsibility of the learner. In the shift from the acquisition of skills and knowledge to high-level problem-solving, collaboration becomes more important too. Complex problems can rarely be tackled alone. Problem-solvers must see how their own knowledge and skills complement those of others. So problem-solving is fundamentally relational. Whether between learners and teachers, learners and peers or learners and the world, relationships are what inspire people to want to solve problems.

A learning environment must therefore create space and purpose, and build connections. With this shift in emphasis, some more principles can be added to the list proposed at the end of Chapter 3:

1. Trust learners to be independent

2. Provide support to learners as they grow in independence, though mentoring and coaching

3. Expand horizons – open up learning to different people, spaces and insights

4. Teach across subject boundaries

5. Be democratic – encourage teachers to listen to and learn from students, and students to listen to and learn from their peers

Finally, as Lucas points out above, people need to be taught how to reflect and to make good choices. This requires a real sense of mission – an understanding of and sense of responsibility for a 'bigger picture'. Daniel Pink, author of *Drive: The Surprising Truth About What Motivates Us*, has reviewed the knowledge base on the subject of motivation and captures it memorably. In his book, he cites decades of scientific research that shows how the most effective way of motivating people is not through the 'carrot and stick' approach, the threat of punishment and the promise of extrinsic reward. Rather, the secret to increased levels of happiness and productivity – at work, at school, at home, and in other spheres of life – lies in tapping into people's intrinsic motivations. He identifies the three most powerful elements of motivation as mastery, purpose and autonomy. [43] These elements provide a useful framework for thinking about the continuum that emerges from the analysis of the innovations in this book: acquisition of relevant skills and knowledge leads to *mastery*. Generating solutions to complex challenges requires and achieves *purpose*. And with mastery and purpose, learners can exercise more *autonomy*, choosing and defining for themselves the problems that require solving, and thereby creating new possibilities for themselves and the world around them. The next chapter looks at how learners across the world are being supported to do just that.

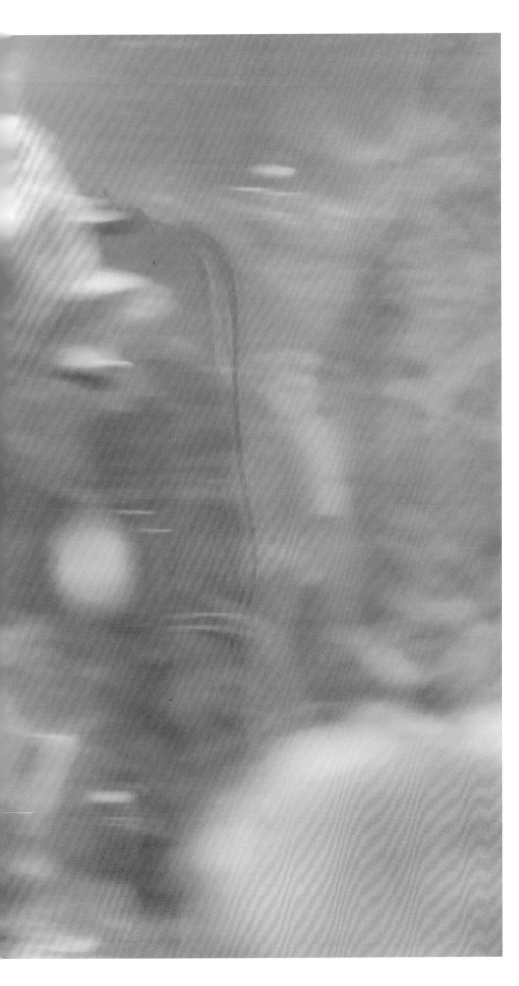

Luna da Costa, fascinated
by the fishtank at Lumiar
School, São Paolo, Brazil.

Sir Fazle Hasan Abed, founder of BRAC and Laureate of the inaugural WISE Prize for Education, 2011, with students at BRAC Primary School in the Korail slum, Dhaka, Bangladesh.

THE CENTER FOR INNOVATION AND ENTREPRENEURSHIP

Student David Delanos displays the bags produced by his business Plant Your Print, in front of the Center for Innovation and Entrepreneurship, Providence, Rhode Island, one of the projects supported by Big Picture Learning.

CHAPTER 5

THE NEXT FRONTIER

Creating possibilities

Innovators have the capacity to see the world differently. Seized by the conviction that the speed with which our world is changing is simply not matched by education systems, they are looking into the roots of the problem and devising new ways to tackle it. Old ways were predicated on a world where we were less globally interdependent and connected, most jobs were low skill/low wage, and the world was shaped for us. Innovators are recognising that not only can they create new possibilities, but that young people can and must be enabled to do so too.

In the USA, this drive and vision have been realised in a growing network of schools designed by Big Picture Learning.

BIG PICTURE LEARNING AT THE MET

Preparing for her graduating high school prom, Cynthia Zapata is as excited as any other North American teen, but she is also reflective as she prepares to leave the institution where she has been educated for the last four years. 'My life didn't start till I came here,' she says. 'This school made me.'

Cynthia's high school progress would not have been predicted from her background. A sickly child, suffering from a rare inherited disease, she spent most of her early life in an incubator or in intensive care. Cynthia's parents are Colombian. Her father came to the US some 30 years ago, her mother subsequently joining them. Cynthia's mother still speaks little English, and Spanish is the language spoken at home, where Cynthia has three siblings. Cynthia was not expected to live long, but she somehow made it through elementary and middle schools. At one point their home burned down, destroying all their possessions. Then came her lucky break: through the lottery admission process she got a place at the Metropolitan Regional Career and Technical Center (the 'Met') in her home city of Providence, Rhode Island.

Through the Met, Cynthia has had the opportunity to experience six internships in a variety of organisations, each one of them occupying two full days of each week of her school career. Her last internship was at the State Attorney General's Office. The work she did there on Identity Theft for Teens has been published and made publicly available. She will study law at the local Roger Williams University and is confident that in due course she will go to graduate law school at Harvard. She will be an immigration lawyer specializing in human rights. She is of course the first in her family ever to attend college.

Although Cynthia is now set upon a legal career, in the course of her time at the Met she has seriously considered a range of other options, including photography and aviation. 'This school is awesome if you don't know what you want to do. Most kids don't.'

The Met is 'awesome' in a number of respects, including its outcomes. It serves twice as many Hispanic students and three times as many African American students as the Rhode Island state average. Sixty-nine percent of its students are eligible for free or reduced-cost school lunch (the best proxy for family poverty) and 42 percent come from homes where English is a second language. Yet, its on-time graduation rate is 90 percent compared to a national average of 69.5 percent; and to other urban averages of 45 percent (New York City), 25 percent (Detroit) and 45 percent (Los Angeles). Moreover 95 percent are accepted into college. There are some hard data too, that capture the level of engagement. In 2009, the Rhode Island Department of Education asked students across the state to take a survey to assess their schools and learning. The Met was more highly rated than other schools in the state in almost every category, particularly in those evidence-based practices known to achieve student success: 87 percent agreed that 'My teachers keep me interested in class' (compared to a 32 percent state average); 57 percent agreed that 'My teachers give me tough problems to solve' (compared to a 43 percent state average).

Underlying these numbers, though, is something even more impressive. The best way to apprehend this is to be amongst and talk to the students. It is rare indeed to talk to high school students from underserved urban communities who are so articulate about how important their school is to them, how it has changed them, how it is creating a future for them. And how much they love it.

Co-Founder and Co-Director Dennis Littky sums up the key insight that has informed his innovative education designs from the outset: 'When young people are given real world experience and their learning is grounded in it, they change. By engaging them and respecting them, you will change them. They become transformed.'

This is by now a familiar theme. Innovators from Finland to Brazil are clear that this real world foundation is critically important – whether learners are building a particular skill set or learning to solve complex problems.

The Met makes this relationship with the world of work fundamental. It is not a bolt-on or additional extra. Nor is it instrumental – a means to raise funds. The entire learning design upon which the Met and its sister schools are based is founded on it. In practice this means that, of every student's five-day week, two days are spent in internships. This year, over 698 internships have been arranged, involving over 500 external mentors. The range is vast: local radio and TV stations; sports orga-

Cynthia Zapata was awarded
the Thairus Rivas Leadership
Award from her school:
'This school is awesome if you
don't know what you want
to do. Most kids don't.'

Brenda de la Cruz, helping
to construct the brand
new Applegate Community
Gardens in South Providence,
Rhode Island. Students
of the Metropolitan Regional
Career and Technical Center
(the 'Met') experience a wide
range of work.

Cesar Breton, an intern
at A&P Auto, Providence,
where he carries out
repairs as well as training
other interns.

Sami Abdellaoui and Lina
El Yakhloufi created
the company YouthYell
as an INJAZ initiative when
they were still at high school.

nisations; hospitals; businesses large and small; cultural organisations; law, finance and professional services companies; the military; new tech; farming. It is hard to think of an aspect of human endeavour that these young people do not have an opportunity to become a part of. Cynthia's work in her Attorney General's Office internship is now in public use. Students are broadcasting, or designing, or serving, *for real*.

A natural extension of this level of engagement with the world of work has been to develop a focus on entrepreneurship. From a basics course – E101 – the school has moved to offering a more intensive programme – E360. Within this, students are educated and supported in all the processes entailed in starting their own businesses, which all of them do. The culmination of this work was the opening, in May 2012, of the first free-standing Center for Innovation and Entrepreneurship in a US high school. In opening the building, Providence's Mayor Angel Tavares not only praised the work but told the students: 'We need you.' Politicians increasingly recognise that the vitality of a thriving entrepreneurial culture is critical to economic regeneration. They will not get this from conventional education.

The new Center provides offices, business back-up, display and meeting space for the students. It aims to create an environment where start-ups will thrive and where students will learn. E360 is intense. Students are selected for it on the basis of their ideas and their commitment. The programme covers all aspects of business start-up and the 'academic' content that underpins it. This includes maths and communication, but many other disciplines as well.

David Delanos – a junior at the Met – has created *Plant your Print* to provide custom-designed and hand-printed canvases for students' backpacks. Jeira Titin – also a junior – owns and runs *Por' Usted Creat*, producing customised healthy cupcakes without sugar or additives, catering for occasions and special tastes. *Spider Software* was created by Angela Murcia to create a new approach to online safety, whilst improving users' online experience. The precursor of all of these was *Big Picture Soda*, started by a group of 12 students (who were part of the pilot of E360 in 1996). The company makes all-natural soda, and has donated over $10,000 to the *Met Dollars for Scholars* programme out of its overall net profit.

The Met School is part of Big Picture Learning, a not-for-profit co-founded by social entrepreneurs Dennis Littky and Elliot Washor in 1995. The principles (or 'distinguishers') of Big Picture infuse all its schools: there are now 52 across America (serving some 9000 students). All are public schools; some operate as public charter schools. Others have been started in Australia, Canada and the Netherlands. The language of the Big Picture principles is now common rhetoric. But they are made real in Big Picture Learning through:

Small personalised classes. At the Met, students are placed in groups of 15 called 'advisories'. They stay in this grouping, with an advisor, for their four years in the school. The advisor gets to know every student really well, and is crucial to creating a powerful learning experience for every student. The Big Picture Learning design seeks to create a mix of classes – small groups, tutoring, online, travel experiences, college classes – to suit individual learning styles and needs.

A curriculum relevant to the real world and built from students' passions. Students work with their advisors to create individual learning plans that blend students' passions and interests with core conceptual content. They are supported by curriculum specialists. Learning is structured around projects that bring in other aspects of curriculum according to the Met's learning goals.

Internships, projects and entrepreneurship are central, not peripheral. Internships are arranged for every student, although often the students work together in groups. Collaborative learning is central to the approach. Two days a week is obviously a huge investment of time. No-one within the school suggests it should be anything less. If a student embarks on E360, then the building of their business in effect becomes their internship.

Small school learning environments. The small advisories are themselves grouped into small schools: the Met comprises six schools, each of 150 students, in separate buildings grouped around a campus. Each school has its own identity and is small enough for students and teachers to build real relationships. The schools share facilities such as fitness, creativity and media, and entrepreneurship.

The impulse that inspired Littky and Washor to innovate in this space was outrage: that so many kids were failed by an expensive, mechanistic system was just not acceptable. Their outrage is now extending to the post-school sector. Littky, a principal in the public school system all his life, has been ignited by the extraordinary statistic that in the US, 89 percent of first-generation college students drop out.[44] And they do so having accrued significant debt. The Met knows that a college degree is a portal to the good life and is foundational for reinvigorating the American economy. It has now launched *College Unbound*. Through this initiative, in partnership with the Rhode Island's Roger Williams University, Big Picture Learning offers three-year degrees grounded in real work: contextually rich and deeply academic. The animating question will always be: what are the skills and knowledge required for today's world?

Big Picture Learning is keen to share and to scale: in addition to the replicated 52 schools in the US and a further 50 worldwide, the Met alone hosts 500 visitors a year.

But this enthusiasm is not reflected in the prevalent policy dynamic – familiar the world over – that emphasises standardisation and 'performance-based' testing in a reductionist concept of 'personalisation'. Washor remarks: 'This is a hard environment to work in. We don't want to run thousands of schools, but we want to have influence. We seem to have more internationally – maybe you have to "take it out to bring it back". And we want to be in a position constantly to innovate.' Next forays in this space include moving to run the complete system for disaffected dropout students ('alternative provision') in Tulsa and Sacramento. Big Picture Learning is an advisory partner to the New York City iZone, which is seeking to create new models of schooling for the city.

Certainly one route to scale could be to develop work still further with the underserved groups at the far end of the spectrum – those who drop out entirely, sometimes at quite young ages. This is what UK innovator Stephen Heppell is doing with his hugely successful Notschool programme, using technologies to build curricula around learners' passions. Both Notschool and Big Picture are creating new paradigms that disrupt the old 'givens' of the system – five days in a schoolhouse with a curriculum determined by others – and end up out-performing the conventional model in the process, *on its own terms.*

Like Omnia, Growth Sector and others, Big Picture Learning stands at the very nexus of academic and vocational traditions. It demonstrates how the two can be integrated in a way that makes sense. The legitimacy of these initiatives derives from the success of their students and the kind of people they become: genuinely ready for college or career, in charge of their own lives, taking responsibility for their actions, and prepared to create possibilities.

Cynthia Zapata, about to leave her high school and embark on her college career, looks thoughtfully across the school campus and considers her future. 'I think… after becoming Governor, I may be the first female Hispanic President.'

————

Back in Finland, InnoOmnia are doing something similar with entrepreneurs of all ages. Mervi Jansson, one of the co-creators of the initiative, remarks:

> We have rightly been very focused in VET in getting *out* to business. And we thought: why not get business *in* too, and make an even greater integration? We didn't want to be just another business park, not just a school for entrepreneurs, not just a college development unit: we're all three.

InnoOmnia mixes age, education and experience; formal and informal learning; physical and virtual spaces. The entrepreneurial hub offers a one-year LUOVIVA-program for young businesses with a focus on service sector start-ups. Special emphasis is on joint projects with students, offering opportunities for on-the-job learning and encouraging students to consider starting their own business after graduation.

The LUOVIVA-program includes business coaching and networking events. When new entrepreneurs join InnoOmnia, they take part in a welcome interview where their specific needs and interests are mapped. There are now 40 businesses involved. Entrepreneurs can take advantage of Omnia shop, an in-house store for entrepreneurs to display and sell their products on campus. Students start project-based learning with InnoOmnia staff, and as their skills develop, move on to more demanding projects and finally get financial compensation for their work.

Annina Cederström and Oskari Nukarinen rent space at InnoOmnia and coach students. They use the network and buzz to develop their business, o+m=g design. They specialise in design and manufacture of household and personal items from recycled materials. Both had come through Omnia's Upper Secondary vocational programme, both worked in other companies for a while, then decided entrepreneurship was the way forward:

> The experience here has helped us develop our business model and change our focus. The rent is reasonable – but the network of entrepreneurs – and students – is so diverse. What do we get here? Expertise, exchange, collaboration … oh, and joy and fun! We love working with the students.

————

An entrepreneurial mindset does not necessarily mean a future creating start-ups or indeed working within business. It is more fundamentally about a spirit of initiative and personal efficacy. However, economists increasingly concur that entrepreneurialism is a major driver of growth and prosperity. Startups in the US create an average of 3 million new jobs annually. All other organisations, from companies in their first full years of existence to firms established two centuries ago, are net job destroyers, losing 1 million jobs net per year. The Global Entrepreneurship Monitor 2011 Report estimates that there were 388 million entrepreneurs actively engaged in starting and running new businesses in 2011. [45]

This is as relevant in stagnant as it is in emergent economies. In many parts of the Middle East and North Africa, the spirit of the Arab Spring continues unabated, with simmering levels of discontent, frequently focusing on unemployment. But this is not just a failure of markets, or a result of corruption. It is in spite of dysfunctional education systems that youth have led inspiring movements for change. The change needs to encompass not just economies, but learning systems too.

Children working on a Round
the World in Eighty Days
project at Lumiar school,
São Paolo.

Bassma Oudda, a student
on the Al Jisr School-Business
Partnerships programme.

AL JISR SCHOOL-BUSINESS PARTNERSHIPS / INJAZ AL MAGHRIB

Mhammed Abbad Andaloussi's appearance is rather misleading. A retired banker, he dresses in sober suits and has the quiet demeanour of one who has worked all his life in the financial sector. Under all this is an urgent determination to transform the life chances of young Moroccans. He fizzes with ideas and seizes upon shadows of possibilities that he might turn into reality. Now a prominent social entrepreneur, Andaloussi is so absorbed in this mission that he literally cannot sleep – managing only three or four hours a night. To the consternation of his family, he is working harder than ever before – and loving it. It has not gone unnoticed. Andaloussi's efforts in setting up Al Jisr and INJAZ Al Maghrib have been recognised by the Schwab Foundation for Social Entrepreneurship (Social Entrepreneur of the Year), the Clinton Foundation (Global Citizen), and the Ashoka foundation. His Al Jisr project was a WISE Award winner in 2011. Notwithstanding all this global recognition he is actually a 'silver revolutionary'.

Andaloussi is the son of a carpenter, the only one in his family of seven to go to university. His motivation is his profound dismay at the opportunities available to young Moroccans as they leave school or college. Young people (14–29) make up 30 percent of the population, and of them, 49 percent are in neither education or employment.[46] The Arab Spring led to early unrest, in response to which the King established a Constitutional Council, signalling his intention to move towards a constitutional monarchy and civil society. How fast and how effectively the government is moving to address the plight of the young unemployed is a matter for debate. Whilst there has been no crowd violence, self-immolation amongst protesting graduates began in 2012: they became known as the *diplômés chômeurs*. Unemployed youth are regularly to be seen in orderly demonstrations, wearing matching smocks and stopping the traffic outside the Parliament building. In a telling move, they have also occupied the Ministry of Education.

The protesters are right to focus on a failing education system. Currently, only 60 percent of the population complete secondary education – the majority of dropouts being in rural areas. As with participants in Lumiar, JCEF and many others, even those who stay do not hold the school system in high regard. To top it off, the common and deep divide between education and business prevails.

Into all of this Andaloussi has brought two initiatives. The first, Al Jisr ('The Bridge'), commits businesses to becoming actively involved with individual schools. Staff from these companies are directly engaged in taking the school forward. They do not just donate CSR money at arm's length.

INJAZ Al Maghrib is affiliated to the wider INJAZ Al Arab movement.

INJAZ's mission is to 'reveal their own potential to young Moroccans and stimulate their spirit of initiative, through the involvement of companies with public education'.

INJAZ has a model for how to make this happen. The idea – as with so many powerful social innovations – is simple. Volunteers from Moroccan companies are trained to work directly with young people. They use materials that INJAZ has adopted and adapted from the Junior Achievement programme, originally established in the US as long ago as 1919. The idea is to introduce students to entrepreneurialism through hands-on learning. Through this, the programme aims to create a changed culture and a different mindset. The programme is open to all public schools in Casablanca, Rabat and Tangier. Among those involved are schools from the most disadvantaged areas.

'We got a chance to live what we dreamed,' said Jihane, who created Assoldy, a company producing 'modern tunics with a traditional touch, made for and by Moroccan women'. In 2009 the company won second prize in the International Youth Enterprise competition.

Sami Abdellaoui and Lina El Yakhloufi created the company YouthYell as an INJAZ initiative when they were still at high school. Both are now students at King Hassan University, studying Infomatics, and have just registered the company which they plan to take to the next level. Ironically it works to bring Moroccan street art (often aimed at expressing protest) to the market. The designs are used on T-shirts, flags, paper and glassware. Street artists can make a living and have their designs more widely distributed. A prize-winner in regional competitions organised by the umbrella INJAZ Al Arab organisation, the company has further developed its business plans and attracted venture funding.

'I have learned to take control of my life,' says Lina. 'I have learned not to stand and watch. In contrast with our other lessons, we had the responsibility. Nobody gave us any solutions. It has changed me completely. I found out that the more you do, the more you can do. I don't want to be an employee now.'

Sami adds: 'In school, the teacher talks, the students listen. Actually, we sleep. It's no better in university. In computer engineering, there's hardly any interaction. Still, we'll endure it, because I think we can use that stuff to help us with what we really want to do. With INJAZ our adviser said: This is serious – but let's make it fun! And it was. We enjoyed it so much. We learned business-planning, marketing, teamworking, management skills. We brainstormed, and learned how to make that work. We thought about how to get the best out of all our team members.'

INJAZ Al Maghrib is now delivering an entrepreneurship module for third-year university students. Mohamed Ouazzani Touhami, Dean of the Casablanca Faculty of Sciences at Morocco's King Hassan University, comments: 'There has been a revolution in this faculty in the last few years. We used to be known as "the faculty of the unemployed". Students are starting to demand different things. Teachers are struggling to learn new methods and adopt a pedagogy of motivation. Professional development is central to that, but we don't have enough resource to support it properly.'

INJAZ is contributing to this professional development. In its entrepreneurship module it models practical learning with business volunteers who adopt a very different approach. Students love it.

The model depends upon the active engagement of business volunteers, of whom it might literally be said, this is not their business. One view is that teachers should teach and business should create wealth and employment. This is not the view of Laila Mamou, the CEO of Wafasalaf, a major financial services group in Morocco. A busy and influential business woman, she nevertheless is a board member of INJAZ, a partner in INJAZ and Al Jisr, and is also a volunteer. She believes that what she puts in, she (and her company) will get back, many times over. For her it is absolutely critical that education and business come closer together and understand more about their relative spheres and areas of expertise. Ms Mamou speaks movingly of the degree to which involvement with the programme expresses not only her aspirations for her company in relation to the future direction of Moroccan society, but also 'my humanity. My deepest values. This is the sort of work that gives meaning to my life'.

Andaloussi has deployed five arguments to engage such a wide swathe of Moroccan business in education. First, the work represents powerful professional development of a company's staff. Second, it changes the image of business from the caricature of greedy predators in an authentic way that CSR programmes cannot match. Third, it improves the loyalty of staff, because they can become involved in something they believe in and they can creatively contribute to. Fourth, companies are contributing to the stability of the country. How do they see the future if nothing changes? And finally, they have – or should have – an interest in preparing the consumer of tomorrow. Does this play?

The Boston Consulting Group (BCG), itself an INJAZ partner, has been conducting a pro bono study of INJAZ's work and contributing to its future strategy. It believes that the arguments are valid, but to achieve the scale-up that Andaloussi aspires to achieve, more evidence is needed. Their analysis is that Morocco's economy is unbalanced: whilst there is a small number of very strong companies, as a whole the economy lacks small and medium enterprises (SMEs). To create them, a fundamental change in culture is needed, a widespread change of mindset. BCG sees INJAZ Al Maghrib as part of the solution, but not just through focusing on and enabling entrepreneurship. The broader

objective is to change the basic approach within classrooms from outmoded and passive to one of deep engagement. In the narrower sense of creating higher levels of entrepreneurship, INJAZ's early evidence looks very promising. Longitudinal studies have not yet been done (and are complex and expensive) but on a conservative estimate, BCG believes that the INJAZ Al Maghrib model could scale in Morocco from the current 5000 students to 15,000 per year within the next five years.

This is nowhere near good enough for Andaloussi. 'My mission is to change, and it's urgent. I know we can spread this faster. If we partnered with government (50–50) we could franchise – but the emphasis needs to be on quality, not just numbers. It must become a part of the curriculum, not an extra-curricular add-on. A social entrepreneur is never discouraged. You just keep persevering. When we are passionate we become contagious.'

———

Andaloussi's remark about the need to integrate entrepreneurship learning into formal education is consistent with emerging insights across the globe. In Japan Koji Omi, former Minister of State, respectively, for Finance, Science and Technology and for Economic Planning, believes that 'The focus in education needs to shift to developing students' abilities to *discover problems* on their own and work out methods of solving those problems on their own too.' Dr Omi touches here on a central point: the 21st century has witnessed a shift in balance from the consumption of knowledge to its creation.

This endeavour cannot be restricted to the issue of knowledge. A recent European Commission Report found that, although entrepreneurship education is provided in most countries, it generally ignores the importance of creating 'entrepreneurial attitudes'. [47] Teaching it as a branch of economic theory will not do. Professor Yong Zhao argues in his 2012 book that cultivating creative and entrepreneurial talents requires a paradigm shift – from employee-oriented education to entrepreneur-oriented learning. [48]

La Bastilla school in Nicaragua suggests that this analysis holds for emerging, as well as advanced economies.

LA BASTILLA TECHNICAL AGRICULTURAL SCHOOL, NICARAGUA

———

Nicaragua is the second poorest country in Latin America. In the Jinotega region where La Bastilla Technical Agricultural School is based, the high school attendance rate is only 20.1 percent. Illiteracy rates are high and education is commonly viewed as an unaffordable luxury: many impoverished families eke out a 'hand to mouth' existence on a small piece of land, and need their children to help out.

Undeterred, Markus Fischer, an experienced Swiss German business-man took charge of the struggling La Bastilla Coffee Estate in 2004. He was determined to set up a secondary school that would be tailored to the needs of the local area, giving the poorest children a route to higher education and better job prospects. Partnerships helped. In 2009, Markus' charity Foundation for Rural Education and Entrepreneurship (FEER) teamed up with Teach a Man To Fish, an NGO that seeks to promote sustainable education projects in some of the world's most deprived areas through grassroots enterprise. Teach a Man to Fish now has global reach, providing financial and technical support to hundreds of schools to create new sources of value that enable the poorest children to attend school for free.

With the help of Teach a Man to Fish, La Bastilla Technical Agricultural School secured funds to set up a series of businesses that would enable the school to become self-sufficient. It now boasts an impressive array of small enterprises, including an eco-lodge (offering guestroom accommodation on the estate), egg, milk and pork production, a small bakery, several vegetable patches, and coffee seedlings that are cultivated in polytunnels and sold to the coffee farm. There have also been businesses that failed, like bee-keeping (the bees fled the hive). Experimentation and failure are inevitable and essential parts of the students' learning. The school is now almost 60 percent self-sufficient and is aiming to be fully self-sufficient by 2015.

The 'learning by doing' methodology is a highly engaging learning model as well as making money. La Bastilla is attended by 38 students aged 15–18. Three days of their school week are devoted to studying academic subjects, and two to practical learning in subjects such as animal and plant production. Each week, groups of students rotate between the various businesses so that they can gain experience of different areas. Most students say they prefer this hands-on, practical approach, particularly when they hear the sales figures at the end of each month – a tangible output of their learning that helps them to feel pride in and ownership of the school.

At La Bastilla, learning is geared towards creating a generation of 'entrepreneurial minds'. As Markus puts it, 'a good idea is worth ten cents. The value comes when you know how to implement it. I wanted to create a school which would enable people to think for themselves at the same time as turning them into highly effective *doers*.' As part of this commitment, the students must complete a business plan in their final year, which they present in front of the whole school. Students are encouraged to think creatively about the resources that they have at their disposal. Which of their family members have a spare field or room that they might be able to use? What organisations might they approach for extra funding or free resources? Amongst last year's graduating class, the best ideas ranged from an internet café using secondhand computers to a bakery and a chicken-fattening business.

The importance of resourcefulness and environmental awareness infuse the educational philosophy and design of La Bastilla. Buildings are powered by solar panel, bio digesters produce methane used in the school, and students learn about good farming practices and natural forms of pest control. These principles are mirrored in the coffee business: considerable work was needed initially to gain a Rainforest Alliance certification for the estate, including an extensive reforestation programme.

This was not done out of sentimentality. Markus recognised that it is common sense to protect the welfare of the people and environment on which your business is dependent, and that consumers will pay a high premium for ethical products. Taylors of Harrogate in the UK are amongst the reputable buyers of their *arabica* coffee, and Markus hopes that the estate will continue to grow its reputation as an ethical brand. As he sees it, people, planet and profit are inextricably intertwined – the 'triple bottom line'.

Developing expertise is also a key component of the learning process at La Bastilla school. After two years, students gain their high school leaving certificate, and in their third year they specialise in a chosen technical area. They help to supervise younger students and graduate as an agricultural *tecnico*. This final year enables them to gain a high level of skill, which often means that they can skip the first and even second year of a five-year university degree. This provides a significant incentive for them to go on to higher education.

The majority of students at La Bastilla hope to go to university. This is remarkable given that many of them come from communities where education is seen as being of limited value. One recent graduate from La Bastilla, 20-year-old Nelson Lanuza, once shared this attitude, but his experience at the school enabled him to see things differently. Nelson's mother is an illiterate housewife, and his father works as a small agricultural producer. Growing up with 10 brothers and sisters, life for Nelson and his family was hard. But Nelson dreamed that he would one day become an agricultural engineer with sufficient skills to earn a good salary. At primary school, he lost sight of that dream: 'I didn't like the school or the teaching,' he says. 'I found it boring. I could not see its relevance to my life.'

Like many children in Nicaragua, Nelson did not go to secondary school.

Students prepare the soil for planting maize at La Bastilla Technical Agricultural school, Nicaragua. Two days per week at the school are dedicated to practical learning in subjects such as animal and plant production.

He dropped out at the age of 11 and followed in his father's footsteps, working as a farm labourer. He might have continued on this path, if it had not been for a fateful incident when he was 15. Nelson fell sick and found himself in hospital, with doctors telling him that he might never fully recover. 'That made me realise that I needed to give myself more options. I was worried about how I would make a living if I could not work as a farm labourer.'

Nelson met Don Cesar, a teacher at La Bastilla, who persuaded him to come to see the school. 'I went to visit and they told me that they would offer me a place as long as I was committed to working hard. So I went home, packed my bags, and the next day I started at La Bastilla as a first-year student. I didn't tell my parents where I was going, I just went.'

After four years out of full-time education, Nelson was nervous about going to La Bastilla, but the decision to do so altered the course of his life. 'I thought I already knew a lot about working in the countryside, but through studying I gained knowledge and experience that would enable me to work more efficiently and productively.' In his final year he specialised in vegetable production, but what he loved most was giving the coffee tours. His face lights up when he speaks about it: his passion for coffee production is evident. 'The tours helped me to see myself not just as someone with something to learn, but as someone with something to teach. I gained confidence through being able to tell people about coffee.'

After graduating in 2011, Nelson got a job as a Coffee Quality Controller in the processing plant, supervising a team of eight. He now earns $250 a month, about double what an agricultural worker of his age typically earns. On Saturdays he studies at a university in the nearby town of Jinotega, a common option in Nicaragua for those who cannot afford to study full-time. He is also taking extra courses in IT and farming co-operatives. He is proud of what he has achieved. 'Only two of my siblings even went to high school. I am the first in my family to go to university. My family never believed that I would stick it out – they are shocked.'

Nelson's success is not unique. Many of those who graduated with him in December 2011 had impressive opportunities lined up: one set up her own accountancy business and another achieved a scholarship to study at a university in New York. Another group of boys, from the indigenous Misquito community, dispersed to their homes to become teachers. It took two days for them to complete the journey, much of it by river. In the north of Nicaragua there is almost no infrastructure, but the students hoped to make use of what they had learned at La Bastilla to transform their communities.

It is very difficult to make a profit from primary agriculture, particularly in a school that is some distance away from the nearest commercial centre. The fact that the eco-lodge is by far the most lucrative enterprise that the school runs, however, is a good lesson in itself – services are generally much more profitable than primary industries. Many of the school's resources have been ploughed into maximising the profits of the eco-lodge. And of course it remains very small scale. ILO economist Raymond Torres believes that in poor countries the key will be learning how to move from small enterprises to medium-sized ones – there is a dearth of these, and they are needed to drive economic growth.

As for Nelson, he is committed to pursuing a successful career in agriculture, but he too has learnt the value of service. Earnest and focused, he simmers with ideas for a future business of his own. 'What I really want to do is set up a business selling agricultural products. But I've noticed that few such businesses combine a service element. With my professional experience, I could give customers advice and follow up with them to see how they're getting on with the product. I could become in effect an agricultural consultant.'

———————

Nelson Lanuza, Cynthia Zapata and Lina El Yakhloufi are representatives of a younger generation looking to do and be a lot more than employees – albeit highly skilled ones. These young people want to shape and create their societies in new ways, ways that are more equitable and more sustainable. They want to define new areas of work not already framed by corporations and organisations.

John Elkington believes that there is an emerging generation of young leaders who are not battered by the rapidly changing world in which they find themselves, but embracing it. They have grown up with the internet and modern media, and are highly effective at using these tools to effect change. The Arab Spring is a striking example of this. These young leaders will be quite different from the current leadership class, and have the potential to usher in a new order. 'At the moment we have a political class which is in disarray and is not sure what its next steps should be. The younger generation are confident, assertive, adaptable. They have access to tools and technologies which enable people to think and behave in ways that were inconceivable only a decade ago. In many ways these are positive developments which could enable radical transformations at the interface between work and learning.'

Writer and journalist Paul Mason shares this view. [49] He argues that 'the graduate without a future' is a human expression of an economic problem: the west's model is broken. It cannot deliver enough high-value work for its highly educated workforce. Yet the essential commodity – a degree – now costs so much that it will take decades of poorly remunerated work to pay for it. However, the activist unemployed graduates he has interviewed have other stories too: they've started an online magazine, or a collective, or a business. They've set up a cafe, or a theatre

Teachers and students
celebrating success
in the Al Jisr School-Business
Partnerships programme.
Teachers are learning a new
pedagogy of motivation.

group, or – as in the Andalusian farm he visited – seized abandoned land and planted vegetables. Mason writes: 'This generation is creating forms of business and commerce, literature and art, that live in the cracks left by shrinking GDP and collapsing credit.'

To create such new possibilities beyond 'the cracks', people certainly need foundational knowledge, technical and digital skills; they also need problem-solving skills of collaboration, critical thinking and creativity. But on top of all this they need a new way of looking at the world – a capacity to 'scan the world and its emergent realities'. [50]

The learning principles that deliver on this are now becoming visible. The foundations were built in Chapter 3 and apply even more urgently here – from real-world learning and building relevant skills, to collaboration and responsibility. Chapter 4 added greater space and independence to exercise critical thinking and creativity. Chapter 5 has contributed the final ingredient – the self-reliance and deep connection with the world that enables learners to perceive urgent new challenges – and to do something about them. As Markus from La Bastilla put it, to move from being 'thinkers to doers'. The final two additions to the list of learning principles are therefore:

1. Enable connection – support learners to build meaningful connections with the world around them

2. Build self-reliance – create environments in which learners have to take decisions and create possibilities for themselves – and which model those processes

Chapter 6 looks at all this from a slightly different angle. Acquiring skills, generating solutions and creating possibilities require a greater sense of control and of responsibility for the world we live in. Some of that comes from great learning models. Much of it comes from the values that we are enveloped in.

At the Global Education Centre, Infosys, Mysore, India, trainers focus on workplace skills.

Young workers with Markus
Fischer at the coffee
tree nursery, La Bastilla.

Nelson Lanuza on the dairy
farm at La Bastilla Technical
Agricultural School, Nicaragua.
'Only two of my siblings
even went to high school.
I am the first in my family
to go to university.
My family never believed
that I would stick it out –
they are shocked.'

An oriental slipper produced by the Al Jisr School-Business Partnerships / INJAZ programme in Morocco, where entrepreneurship is integrated into formal education.

CHAPTER 6

UNLOCKING THE VALUE
OF LEARNING

How innovators are accounting for values and changing societies

I actually think that the core problem is education. We need people who can benefit society. But that doesn't seem to be the education system's priority.

Chenchen Lu
19-year-old student, SUSTC

You can train and educate people to do 'x', but unless the system incentivises and rewards certain behaviours, all you will have is a lot of frustrated people. 'Learning' in and of itself is not enough, because people operate within systems and cultures. You need to focus on changing the systems and cultures as much as equipping people with skills and knowledge.

John Elkington
Founding Partner and Executive Chairman of Volans, Interview May 2012

Shodh Yatra is an Indian phrase meaning 'learning walks'. Professor Anil Gupta, founder of the Honey Bee Network and Executive Vice Chair of India's National Innovation Foundation, regularly practices such walks, taking groups of local and international people around different regions of India. They go in the summer and the winter, walking an average of 250 kilometres, passing through unheard-of villages and meeting all manner of people, old and young. The walks are part of a search for new insights, innovations and creativity. These range from new methods of farming to nutritional recipes and the medicinal properties of local flora and fauna. They have been developed through experience and over time, often in adverse circumstances, in remote parts of India. In the evenings, 'night meets' are held, where walkers and villagers convene to share what they know in a ritual cross-pollination of ideas.

On these walks, learning can come from many different sources – from peers, from nature, from creative communities, and from 'the teacher within'. For Gupta, this is important, because in his opinion 'the creation and affirmation of knowledge is controlled by a small section of the global population, often with a vested interest in the preservation of the status quo'. Opening up the knowledge economy to traditionally marginalised groups and neglected sources – what Gupta calls 'faceless innovators' – is vital if we are to challenge the way things are. As part of his work for the Honey Bee Network, Gupta scopes, documents and assesses grassroots innovators in a number of different countries. He connects them with industry experts and access to funding. The work is driven by a strong desire to build a more equitable society, one in which 'traditional knowledge producers at the top of society recognise the potential contribution of those at the bottom'.

The *Shodh Yatra* are designed to demonstrate the importance of learning through observation, interaction and empathy. As Gupta sees it:

> Students are rarely encouraged to change the way they live their own lives based on the mistakes of their predecessors. They are not taught to take accountability for societal problems but are instead taught that they are separate from them. As a result, the potential for social feedback to affect how we make decisions is lost and the mistakes of the past are repeated.

Gupta believes that learning should encourage us to connect emotionally with our surroundings and ask ourselves how far we are implicated in the issues that we see. He summarises the problems that otherwise may arise: 'We know a lot, we feel very little and we do even less.'

What bearing does this have on the innovators and innovations that are teaching people how to 'learn a living'? All of the innovators in this book

attach huge importance to addressing the *values* their learners live by. They seek to impact upon the broader cultural norms in which people live and work – from Smallholder Farmers Rural Radio in Nigeria, which teaches adult farmers to value happiness, health and hygiene, to young staff at Brazil's Lumiar primary schools, who encourage students to be 'more reflective', and the Rising Sun team in California who are working hard to build a young workforce that is passionate about tackling climate change. Most of these innovators are not simply attempting to transmit an ideal set of values – education systems around the world have done this for centuries. Rather, they are redefining what it means to participate in society.

This might strike some observers as a surprising finding in a book about how learning can better prepare people for work, since the success of practical, vocational learning and training has often been narrowly defined by the success with which it prepares people for productive and profitable activity. In many cultures, the perception of vocational learning as little more than a functional and technical pursuit has spawned the attitude that it is inferior to more academic, intellectual pursuits – 'learning for learning's sake'. Sociologist Richard Sennet in *The Craftsman* offers a compelling counter-argument to this by exploring the inherent value of doing good work. As he writes in his conclusion, 'The working human animal can be enriched by the skills and dignified by the spirit of good craftsmanship.' He defines craftsmanship broadly as any practical work – whether carpentry, scientific discovery or parenting – that is not merely carried out as a means to an end, but is rather driven by a habit of commitment, curiosity and questioning and that seeks excellence as its ultimate goal. For Sennett, approaching one's work through a 'subtle interplay between tacit knowledge and self-conscious awareness' can provide people with insights into how to engage with the world at large, and how to explore broader ethical questions. [51] Most of the innovators in this book see their task as being not simply about equipping learners with the ability to work, but teaching and supporting people to be active and engaged citizens who *challenge* society and think, see and behave in ways that *change* it for the better.

In several cases, they are doing this in direct opposition to the prevailing status quo within the countries in which they are based. This is strikingly true of SUSTC in China, where the dominant political and education systems are still characterised by convention and compliance, while a newly rich, younger generation is beginning to enjoy the heady freedoms of flashy cars and new technologies. One professor of physics made the point that 'we should be teaching these young people how to be good people too', but shyly wondered: 'Is it too much to expect a small university like this to change things?'

Values of course define and change societies. If they are to do so for the good, people from all walks of life – poor and rich, young and old, marginalised and gentrified – must feel a sense of responsibility and a will to act. They must also have the practical support and enablement to do so. Without these ingredients, a young person might worry about climate change but not feel able or impelled to do anything about it; a retiree might wish to continue learning in old age but not see it as appropriate; or a woman working in a factory in Bangladesh might see her male colleagues earning twice as much as her as unfair, but feel powerless to change the situation. What are innovators around the world doing to encourage values-based learning and action, and what are the issues that they are responding to?

WHAT VALUES, AND WHY?

SELF-RESPECT FOR WIDOWS IN GHANA

At the open-air conference centre in Accra, Ghana, 2000 widows are having a lot of fun. They have come from all over the country. Some wear veils, others crosses. Some are exuberant and laughing, others are quiet and withdrawn. Some wear T-shirts bearing the name of their widows' group, others wear traditional dress. The youngest is 20. The oldest is 95. What unites them every day is the death of their husbands and their subsequent ejection from society. What unites them on this particular day is their joy at being together, at singing and dancing, and at meeting the famous Akumaa Mama Zimbi, founder of the Mama Zimbi Foundation and of the Widows' Alliance Network (WANE).

Widowhood in Ghana is seen as a curse. Women are traditionally blamed for their husbands' death, regardless of whether they were in the same State, let alone the same house at the time. Many are branded as witches. The late husband's family will seize any property and assets. The women will not be allowed to take part in any funeral or memorial. They will not wash or eat. They are left to care for their children with no resources and no self-respect.

While hosting a TV chat show and radio broadcasts on the subjects of marriage, love and sex, Mama Zimbi – whose real name is Mrs Joyce Akumaa Dongotey-Padi – would receive text messages, emails and phone calls from widows who were listening and watching. They told painful stories of their loss – not just of their husbands, but of their lives, houses and self-belief. 'Their stories were heart-breaking,' she says. Women talked about how their children would often end up leaving school to work or enter into child marriage to try and help. One woman was dragged through the mud as punishment for her partner's stroke. In 2007, Mama Zimbi was driven to establish the Widows' Alliance Network out of a strong sense of social injustice and a desire to emancipate widows.

As part of this work, the organisation arranges an annual conference that brings together widows from all over Ghana in a united act of defiance.

The room rises to its feet as Mama Zimbi addresses the conference for the first time. The women wave their white handkerchiefs, sway to the music and chant 'Medaase!', Mama Zimbi's famous catch phrase. It means, simply, thank you. It is a statement of appreciation, meaning that who you are and what you have done matters. She encourages mothers to say it to their children, and children to their mothers. For Mama Zimbi, 'Medaase' is the foundation of a new society in which we all take more notice of each other and value each other's contributions. This might be at home, at work or in the marital bedroom. The next part of WANE's work involves providing women with the emotional and practical support to become financially self-reliant. The organisation supports local widows' groups to identify small businesses that might be viable in their area, and provides them with training in the skills they will need to make it happen. 'We are not interested in education in theory – there has to be an avenue to practice for it to have impact.'

Lydia, from Northern Accra, is involved in a local group that has set up a small soap-making factory. The Mama Zimbi Foundation provided both a start-up loan and training to get it going. Other groups produce *gari* or *kenke* (staple foods made of cassava and cornmeal) and palm oil. This practical work does something more than helping widows to make money. It gives them confidence and a focus other than their grief. For older ladies in particular – without children – it also breaks up the debilitating loneliness. Even when they are not working, they are sitting with the younger women, singing, talking and encouraging them.

But the first crucial lesson that WANE teaches widows is that we must value ourselves and our capabilities before we can contribute to the world around us. Without self-respect, widows in Ghana remain the pariahs of society, poor, victimised and powerless.

RECIPROCITY FOR ELDERLY PEOPLE IN JAPAN

In a quite different context, several thousand miles away, the world's tallest TV tower has just opened in Sumida in north-eastern Tokyo. Cameras flash and tills ping as tourists flock to this formidable new addition to the landscape, a 2080-metre-tall construction of glass and steel that towers above the traditional slanting roofs and serene shrines that characterise this part of town. In this country of many paradoxes, old and new are often harmoniously juxtaposed.

Down below, in the shadow of this dazzling obelisk, five retirees are gearing up for an afternoon of work. They are members of the local Silver Human Resource Centre (SHRC), a network of government-sub-

FOLLOWING PAGES

Widows from the Widows' Alliance Network, Ghana.

Members of the Silver Human Resource Centres, Japan.

sidised organisations in Japan that make it possible for retirees aged 60 and above to carry out community-based, part time paid work and to learn on a flexible basis. First established in 1974, they now boast more than 800,000 registered members.

This particular team of five, called 'The Hospitality Team,' spend four hours walking around Sumida three times a week, each time covering a distance of eight kilometres. They wear matching outfits and identical caps displaying symbols of the earth. Their job consists mainly of picking up litter, gardening and giving directions to tourists. The attention to detail and care with which they execute their 'duties' is impressive. Not even the smallest piece of litter goes unnoticed, while every passerby is treated to a cheery greeting. Hospitality is not just a job description for them but a code of conduct, a way of being.

One 67-year-old, Sakumo Sensei, pauses to remove a dead petal from a colourful hanging basket of flowers. Like many of the members of the SHRC, she has come from a highly skilled professional background, having worked before retirement for the education authorities. Why does she want to do this job? 'It keeps me active, both mentally and physically,' she explains. 'I've learnt a lot about this area, for example, and that's been rewarding. You see this flower here? It's the *tsutsuji* – Sumida's flower.'

Silver Human Resource Centres were first set up by the Japanese government as a response to the perception that community cohesion was in decline. Kazuo Ohkouchi, a famous Japanese sociologist, was influential in their design; he believed that their mission should be to instill in retirees four key qualities: independence, autonomy, collaboration and reciprocity. It was hoped these would serve elderly people well in their later years, helping them to stay active, healthy and connected. The government works in partnership with local businesses and public organisations to procure part-time work opportunities, which they then assign to SHRC members. Most are routine and low-skilled, including cleaning up parks, distributing pamphlets, as well as general office tasks and childcare. In recent years the nature of the work opportunities has begun to change to include more high-skilled jobs like IT and translation work. Some centres offer training to 're-skill' retirees in these emerging types of work, and often act as bustling hubs of community activity. Retirees serve as champions as well as beneficiaries of lifelong learning, running workshops on aspects of Japanese culture, such as flower-arranging and cooking.

There is no city in Japan which does not now have a Silver Human Resource Centre. If retirees want to learn and work, they can – and a large proportion of them do. In the years since the foundation of the first centre in Tokyo, the need for elderly people to contribute to society has become more urgent – Japan now faces the world's most rapidly ageing population. The figures are startling: it is predicted that over-65s will account for 40 percent of the population by 2060. [52] But the success of the centres is largely driven by a now broadly held attitude that elderly people should be active participants in society, not by the statistics. Asked whether or not they will continue working through the Silver Human Resource Centres, a large majority of those close to retirement do not hesitate to respond. 'Of course!' they say. The notion that you 'help yourself by helping others' in old age is now firmly entrenched in the collective psyche. As Sakumo sensei says, 'My main motivation for doing this job is to take care of my health. I walk 8 kilometres a day: it keeps me active. But I also have an interest in keeping this area clean. I am proud of Japan and I want to play a role in preserving its beauty.'

YOUNG PEOPLE'S COMMITMENT AND SERVICE TO OTHERS IN KUWAIT

In Kuwait, oil accounts for roughly 50 percent of GDP and 95 percent of government income. [53] Little has been done to diversify the economy, and the oil is running out. No one is quite sure how quickly this will happen, but there is widespread agreement that something needs to be done. Government passed an economic development plan in January 2012 pledging to spend $130bn in five years to diversify the economy. But it cannot happen without a motivated and skilled workforce and the leadership qualities to take the country forward. Kuwait is a young country: 43 percent of the population is under 30. Many of its young citizens are bored, unmotivated and aimless. Young people have money and free time. But many lack purpose and vocational awareness and find themselves drifting into the public sector in which all citizens are guaranteed a job. More than half of Kuwaiti inhabitants are foreign workers.

The Lothan Youth Achievement Centre (LoYAC) was founded in 2002. Not coincidentally, this was just after 9/11. The founders, seven Kuwaiti women, were seized by the realisation that all of the terrorists were under 30. They determined to do something within their own sphere to promote peace by working with young people. Fareah Al Saqqaf is the formidable leader of the Board, and Managing Director. She is uncompromising:

> We felt our country was going backwards instead of advancing. We were becoming more closed to the world, and we needed to become more open. We wanted to do something that enabled young people to find themselves, to become employable, to find peace. We wanted to do something that combined community service and internship – the community service part is vital. Through that, you can extend yourself to others, learn to relate to others.

The resulting non–profit organisation caters to youth between 6 and 28 years of age. It is headquartered in Kuwait but has chapters in Jordan and Lebanon. Through forging partnerships with public and private

LoYAC intern Shahad Al Aseri,
preparing the children's room
at the Asnan Clinic, Kuwait.
LoYAC partners with public
and private organisations
to create opportunities for
young people.

Rehearsal at the LoYAC
Academy of Performing Arts.
Part of the cultural programme
aims to foster values through
an emphasis on the arts.

LoYAC intern Razan Al Huneidi
at work at the reception desk,
Sheraton Hotel, Kuwait City.

organisations, LoYAC creates opportunities for young people to do community service and internships, and supports them to get the most out of these opportunities. 'LoYAC know how to prepare students well for this kind of experience,' says the HR manager of Zain, a major player in the Middle East telecoms industry. 'They come well prepared and in the right frame of mind. We trust them. They show higher levels of leadership. They know the value of what we do.'

LoYAC is a small organisation in a small country, but its holistic and creative approach to the 'sleeping problem' of disengaged youth should be of general interest. This problem will not lead to riots on the street, but it could leave the country adrift, without a motivated workforce able to skill and reskill itself to meet the challenges of the later part of the 21st century. LoYAC's vision is to empower Arab youth to lead their communities towards peace and prosperity. The two are indissolubly linked. And they require new values.

DEVELOPING VALUES: WHOSE RESPONSIBILITY?

The Widows' Alliance Network, Silver Human Resource Centres and LoYAC are all very different organisations operating in very different contexts. They are all explicitly setting out to do two interrelated things: develop human capital and enable a 'contribution' to society through new norms and values. This means self-respect for widows in Ghana, reciprocity for retirees in Japan, commitment and service to others for young people in Kuwait. The idea that individuals need to be more accountable for themselves and the way they live their lives connects all three of these innovations. This is as true for Kuwait's privileged young people needing to be weaned off reliance on an overindulgent public sector as it is for Ghana's widows. 'Did you bury your hands along with your husband?' Mama Zimbi asks of the widows who are mourning their loss, in an attempt to galvanise them into action. In other words, helping people to be more effective and productive contributors to society goes hand in hand with building societies that are more equitable, sustainable, cohesive, and peaceful.

Many of the innovators in this book are responding to contexts that highlight the importance of living and working differently. Where does the responsibility for bringing about these changes lie? Of course, values are strongly influenced by the multiple spheres in which people move through their lives: the families they grow up in, the work they do, the friends they hang out with, the cities they live in, and what they watch on TV. Howard Gardner suggests that in some countries, like the US, creati-

vity is 'in the air and on the streets'. Whether in Hollywood, Silicon Valley or on Wall Street, creativity is visibly exercised and lauded. But prevailing attitudes within these different spheres can also influence people negatively. In Ghana, it is now illegal for a widow to have her property and assets taken away, but the cultural pressures are often so strong that legality is irrelevant. In Kuwait, apathy may breed amongst circles of friends. What kinds of players in society have the power to change such deeply embedded behavioural norms and values?

Some innovators point to education as the root of the problem – and the place for a solution. At 2iE, Lumiar, SUSTC and Big Picture Learning, the very business of these institutions is to build young people equipped with the skills, values and confidence to shape the world around them. Values of self-reliance and responsibility are reinforced in every interaction – in how people relate to each other, the behaviour that is rewarded and the self-direction expected of students pursuing their own learning. But these are outliers. They are pioneers trying to improve upon standards and conventions they see as wholly inadequate. Anil Gupta sees education systems as having failed to encourage people to reflect on past mistakes and take accountability for the world's problems. His learning walks are one method of calling for 'a new way of learning' that is more solidly grounded in the importance of values and taking responsibility. In Kuwait, schools do a reasonable job on basic literacy and numeracy, but the curriculum is narrow, and 'getting the grades' is the main focus. No-one is paying much attention to the engagement and sense of purpose required to reshape an economy and a society. LoYAC is attempting to fill that gap.

LIFELONG LEARNING

Formal education is not the only channel through which values can be shaped and sustained. WANE in Ghana and the SHRCs in Japan deal with groups who have already passed through school and university, or indeed – as with the widows in Ghana – may not have attended school at all. They are examples of organisations providing lifelong learning opportunities. According to Dr Arne Carlsen, Director of UNESCO's Institute for Lifelong Learning (UIL), lifelong learning stands to play an increasingly important role in the education and re-education of people and societies. As he sees it, 'No society today can afford to provide learning only through formal education systems.' He predicts that the major shift over the next 20 years will be from 'education policies' to 'lifelong learning policies'. Advocating values-based lifelong education is a key strategic priority of UIL: all learning activities must be founded on and transmit the principles of peace, democracy, tolerance, intercultural understanding and equity. Jacques Delors' 1996 report to UNESCO's International Commission on Education for the Twenty-first Century, *Learning: the Treasure Within*, remains a key touchstone for the UIL's education policies, and emphasises the importance, in a globally interdependent world, of creating learning communities 'in which everyone plays a part in constructing a responsible and mutually supportive society that upholds the fundamental rights of all'. [54]

Dr Carlsen believes there is a role for political, economic and community leaders to put the systems and incentives in place to enable people to take advantage of such learning opportunities. South Korea, for example, has emerged as a market leader in encouraging lifelong learning, having invested considerable resources in the creation of numerous 'Lifelong Learning Cities'. It has also developed a Credit Bank System (CBS) that accredits diverse learning experiences gained not only in school but also out of school. When a student gains the necessary CBS-approved credits, he or she can obtain an associate or bachelor's degree. Part of a broader strategy to guarantee the global competitiveness of the population, CBS aims to raise the standards of non-formal education and to promote educational self-achievement. Additionally, in South Korea as well as many other countries, efforts to inspire a habit of lifelong learning in citizens include impressive 'lifelong learning festivals'. These enable local providers of informal learning to exhibit their offerings amidst other celebratory arts and cultural events.

The media are other key players who can influence values. Whilst there can too often be a disparity between media messages and societal needs, the power and pervasiveness of the media – and the related world of celebrity – can be harnessed in beneficial ways. In Ghana, one of Mama Zimbi's biggest assets is that by hosting popular radio programmes and TV shows, she has become something of a national treasure. Women at the Widows' Conference queue for an hour at the end of a very long day to say goodbye to her personally. When lunch does not arrive at 4:00 pm, she is able to rouse a tired room just by leading everyone in song through a red microphone with a big 'M' (for 'Medaase') on it.

This popularity and profile is of real importance. As Mama Zimbi says, the generations-old message that widowhood is a curse – and that you are not worthy of a life after your husband is gone – is deeply embedded. 'I have to hit at the same place over and over for it to sink in.' So she says it on her TV show, her radio show, on visits to local widows groups, on her website, blog, and of course at the conference. She hopes that the effect is 'like a bell. Ringing when women go to bed. Reminding them that there is hope and their life is of value.'

LEARNING AT WORK

Many people point to big business as a source of impoverished values in society – profit trumps all. But in some organisations, change is already underway. Rising Sun is one example of the growing number of businesses

modelled on the concept of 'blended value'. Innovative leaders are also emerging to champion the move towards more sustainable forms of business, such as The World Business Council for Sustainable Development, which attempts to galvanise and support CEOs to lead the way.

This trend is not limited to business leaders in the developed world. Infosys takes a highly innovative approach to its employees' development. This includes a strong emphasis on values, captured by 'CLIFE' – Infosys's value statement – which is famous not just within the organisation but throughout the whole of India. CLIFE stands for Customer focus, Leadership by example, Integrity and transparency, Fairness, and Excellence in execution. Trainees spend an entire induction day learning about CLIFE and there is an annual competition for the employees best exemplifying it. It is rare that a conversation goes by without someone referring to it.

'There is a famous story about our founder,' says an employee called Siddarth, referring to Infosys' co-founder Narayana Murthy. 'When they first started the company in 1981, they had to import some computers. The computers got stuck in customs. Officials held up the delivery expecting a bribe to move it along. It never came. They waited for six months. In the end they had to let the computers through. Now, people know that Infosys doesn't do bribes. So they don't bother asking.'

For Infosys' leaders, these values are as much about the development of India as they are about the development of the company. They see the organisation as a platform for social change. This might be through the Campus Connect programme that trains non-Infoscions using their learning model, the SPARK programme that aims to raise the aspirations of children in rural India, or simply the decent pay and good conditions of jobs for the local community at their Global Education Centre.

For businesses, there is another important benefit of embracing positive values: it makes people *want* to work for you. 'I always wanted to work for Infosys,' enthuses Siddharth. Like many of his colleagues, he is not only motivated to keep working hard because he will have a well-paid, well-respected job at the end of it. He is intrinsically proud to be an 'Infoscion'. To return to Daniel Pink's framework noted in Chapter 4, Infosys' values give its workers a powerful sense of purpose. The same might be said of the Silver Human Resource Centres, whose members often work in teams, wear uniforms, and fulfill roles as teachers, caregivers, local ambassadors and guardians of cultural heritage – jobs that are intended to benefit their local areas. The work can be quite menial, but this is almost beside the point – SHRC members are visible and respected figures in their communities. They are seen – and see themselves – as part of a 'social movement'. Studies consistently reflect the fact that, on average, SHRC members have significantly higher levels of health and wellbeing than non-members, making them better able to contribute to society. The benefits of structuring learning and work opportunities so that they harness people's intrinsic motivations cut both ways.

The combination of meaningful learning and work opportunities with the right set of values forms a powerful cocktail for positive behavioural and cultural change. As this chapter has shown, a wide range of people and organisations – from schools and community leaders to workplaces and radio stations – increasingly see it as necessary to bring about this kind of wide-reaching change. But values are deeply entrenched and reinforced every day – and they are not always socially positive. How are the innovators described here developing different, better values in learners, and working to mobilise them? Some common strategies for developing the conditions that allow positive values to grow and flourish are outlined below.

CHANGING AND MOBILISING VALUES

LEAD BY EXAMPLE

Mama Zimbi uses her biggest assets to help change the mindset of Ghana's widows – her charisma, her reach, and the trust and respect she is held in. 'I have to be a role model. I don't drink, I don't smoke, I have good morals - I do what I say. It's important. They trust me.'

Similarly, at Infosys, CLIFE's power is founded on actions as well as words. Prit, who works in Infosys' Human Resources department, proudly recounted a story of internal customer focus – how they had streamlined the welcome and room allocation process for new employees on arrival at GEC. Endless folklore about Murthy refers to his leading by example – his office is said to be like a library. 'He is a rock star for ethical hard work,' says one Infoscion. Integrity and transparency are reinforced through a system of self-governance on campus. Fairness is embedded in a family-friendly – and highly unusual – flexible working policy for mothers. A commitment to excellence is in evidence everywhere you look – from the beautiful gardens to the biggest corporate library in India and the letters home to families that congratulate trainees on their performance. This is just the tip of the iceberg. From courageous professors at SUSTC to collaborative employees at Rising Sun, individuals and organisations are modelling as well as teaching the values that they wish to see in their learners and employees. As one professor at SUSTC remarked, 'We're walking the walk, not just talking the talk.'

BE INCLUSIVE

Another important principle, which underpins many of the innovations in this book, is one of inclusiveness, and the attitude that everybody has the potential to contribute to society positively. No matter how young or old, disadvantaged or deprived, everyone has the power to teach, learn and do. At the Lumiar schools in Brazil, staff do not use well-worn phrases that describe children as 'the leaders of tomorrow' or 'Brazil's future doctors and scientists', because such language defers their value to some unidentifiable future date, overlooking the fact that children have enormous value in and of themselves, *as children*. A philosophy of inclusiveness and equality is also fundamental to the Silver Human Resource model, where elderly people from all sorts of backgrounds can undertake learning and part time work. In Musashino, an outer suburb of Tokyo, 78-year-old Ueno Sensei – a former software specialist for Fujitsu – can be found teaching an IT class to a young woman from the local town, having received some informal teacher training from the Silver Human Resource Centre. 'Oh no, I don't do it for the money,' he chuckles. 'I just thought – well I have all these skills which I built up throughout my career, so why shouldn't I share them?'

ENABLE LEARNERS TO 'OBSERVE, INTERACT AND EMPATHISE'

For LoYAC, the main challenge is the apathy and lack of focus that characterise the mindset of many young people in Kuwait. And there is a pervasive attitude that work in the service sector is looked down upon.

How does LoYAC address this? The organisation's 16 free programmes combine internships, volunteering, a summer programme, leadership development activities, creative programmes in drama and music, and careers and vocational advice. Sport is also seen as a motivator – LoYAC is an AC Milan Soccer Academy, with a club for girls. These programmes give learners a new lens through which to see the world. They put young people in new, unfamiliar situations with different combinations of people. It adds authenticity to their learning experience and – to return to Gupta's terminology – the opportunity to 'observe, interact and empathise'. The effect that this has on young people is dramatic. As Dari, a former LoYAC member, explains: LoYAC has given me so many opportunities to see things differently. At university, you're spoon-fed. No challenge, no responsibility. We need a new way of learning. I had an internship with ExxonMobil, and that, along with the many other opportunities I've had here, changed things for me.'

As Professor Gupta believes, encouraging learners to reflect on and engage empathetically with the world is critical if we are to change society for the better. From new perspectives – 'seeing things differently' – comes a sense of challenge and responsibility. And from challenge and responsibility, comes action. It is telling that Dari now runs his own restaurant, and was also instrumental in setting up LoYAC's K4K (Kuwait for Kenya) programme, a community service programme that highlights the value of volunteer contribution in some desperate communities.

THINK GLOBAL

At InnoOmnia in Finland, they have an excellent phrase for people who embrace this value: 'Born global'. This refers to the importance of seeing yourself not just as a member of a community or even a nation, but as a citizen of the world; to be conscious, for example, of the fact that those in the developing world are suffering from the effects of climate change even while you, in a different country on the other side of the globe, enjoy a perfectly normal life. Narayana Murthy, Infosys' co-founder, has published a set of his speeches as a book, entitled *A Better India: A Better World*. [55] He sees Infosys as part of a holistic picture which, in building a better India also has the potential to build a better world. Many of the innovations in this book explicitly incorporate a similar insight.

BUILD MOVEMENTS OF LEARNERS

The idea that change can be driven by movements of people who identify with one another is not new. The uniform-clad members of the Silver Human Resource Centres and the Rising Sun teams who each summer carry out energy retrofits of people's homes are in large part motivated by a strong sense of shared purpose centred around doing social good. The power of collective learning has been put to effective use by Mama Zimbi in Ghana. She insists on working with *groups* of widows as opposed to individuals. When a woman approaches her from a new area with a tale of appalling treatment, Mama Zimbi's response is to ask her to put together a local widow's group. She will then visit that group herself and introduce them to the WANE principles. This is critical for ongoing mutual support and strength – particularly when new widows join. Local widows' groups can play a critical role in encouraging a new widow to stand her ground and refuse to leave her house, or in helping her go to the police station and get help. Often this simple step can have a profound impact. It takes the whole community to learn for an individual's learning to have meaning. Collective learning leads to collective action.

MAKE IT FUN

From the celebratory learning festivals in South Korea to the parties that Rising Sun holds at the beginning and end of its summer programme, the message is clear: being active and engaged does not have to be boring.

On the contrary, students in the Moroccan INJAZ programme stressed the fun they had, in addition to the hard work. Fun is the overarching theme of the fourth annual Widows Alliance Network conference. The subject matter may be desperately serious and at times very distressing – but how it is communicated is uplifting, vibrant, joyous and energizing. There is a dancing competition around popular, local club tunes. It is not just the youngest women who take part. Women of 50, 60 and 70 lead the celebration with their whole bodies, dancing in the aisles and at one point enveloping the keynote speaker – a popular Ghanaian reverend – in a gyrating mob. As Mama Zimbi stresses, 'You have to make it fun.'

CREATE STRUCTURES THAT PROMOTE POSITIVE VALUES

As John Elkington's remark emphasises at the beginning of this chapter, what good is the desire to contribute in positive ways if there are no opportunities to do so? While increasing numbers of prestigious institutions such as Cambridge University, MIT and Wharton Business School are now providing interesting courses on business, sustainability and ethics, Elkington believes that this will only lead to frustration, as bright-eyed graduates keen to put their learning into practice find themselves in a working world in which profit-driven businesses care little for the issues that they have been educated to tackle. And yet, as already noted, there is a small but growing number of progressive businesses committed to positive social change. Along with the likes of Narayana Murthy, for example, another notably forward-thinking CEO is Unilever's Paul Polman. Under his leadership, the company has recently developed a system of 'environmental profit and loss accounting', making it one of the first businesses to put a market valuation on its carbon footprint. It is now urging other businesses to follow suit. 'These changes may sound technical,' says Elkington, 'but in fact they are profoundly educational.' Businesses are transforming their institutional structures to promote the emergence of a different set of values.

Professor Qingshi Zhu, President of SUSTC, is seeking to achieve something similar in China's academic institutions. In a recent speech, he regretted that the higher education system in China is governed by a hierarchical and bureaucratised system that places too much emphasis on fame and status. He believes that this can compromise the quality of higher education, as scholars become 'disconnected from the real substance of teaching and research' in the constant pursuit of promotion and ever higher levels of funding. When he shared this concern with a group of junior faculty members, however, one staff member commented: 'President Zhu, I couldn't agree with you more, but I have a wife and a child, and it will cost an enormous amount of money to get my child through school. How can I support my family without awards and promotion?' For Professor Zhu, the answer lies in the need to reform higher education in every area, from senior management structures to curriculum design, and to reward staff for their commitment to ethics, innovation and excellence. At SUSTC, he hopes to create an institution that serves as a paragon of academic integrity, where both staff and students are chiefly driven by passion for and dedication to their work, rather than the promise of credentials and other extrinsic factors.

———————

Preparing learners for work and life in the 21st century is not just about matching skills effectively, developing problem-solvers or supporting learners to create their own possibilities. While these help people to contribute to society, enable people to carve their own paths, and build autonomy, mastery, and purpose, they do not, alone, enable learners to change societies for the better. That involves values. It involves having a moral and ethical compass, the courage to go against the grain, to challenge prevailing assumptions, standards, and cultural norms, to learn throughout one's life and through one's work, and to be motivated to do something about the issues that exist in the world – not simply to know about them. Can people 'learn' these values and behaviours? Yes, they can. But not through a textbook, nor through a simple mission statement. It is not a question of passing a test. They have to see, feel and hear the clarion call for change. They have to meet the right people. They have to walk. They have to sing. They have to celebrate. They have to reflect. They have to admire and to aspire. They have to believe themselves capable of effecting change. This is learning in the very broadest sense, and it can happen through a conversation, a dance, work experience, a song, a radio station. The innovators in this book see their job as transformation, not just education. In accounting for values, they are changing societies.

Skills and abilities provide the tools for change, while values empower people and steer them in the right direction. Learning in the 21st century must be a vehicle for all these things.

**Silver Human Resource
Centre members collecting
rubbish in Tokyo, Japan.**

A Silver Human Resource
Centre member at work
at the base of Tokyo's new
TV tower.

Students in BRAC
Primary School, Manikganj,
33 kilometres from
Dhaka City, Bangladesh.

Printing cloth at Ayesha
Abed Foundation, Manikganj,
Bangladesh. The foundation,
a BRAC initiative, employs
65,000 workers, of which
85 percent are women.

Sales girls at Aarong,
a BRAC social enterprise.

CHAPTER 7

THE WHOLE PICTURE

When values and powerful learning come together

(Here) I learn all the ingredients of life. Empathy, communication, dealing with marital stress, and to know myself. I don't learn these things anywhere else.

Nandita
Student, 15, BRAC adolescent programme, Bangladesh

The welcome on walking into a BRAC school is resounding – forty smiling children in red, pink, blue and yellow clothes scrabbling to their feet and all practicing their English to say 'hi' at the tops of their voices. The display of their skills, knowledge and enthusiasm for school life is non-stop. An eight-year-old group leader rallies her troops of four or five other children to do a choreographed, traditional dance to a song about true love. The whole class takes part in a noisy game of 'capital cities', throwing country names, in rhythm, to the next participant to name the capital. What do they want to be when they grow up? Doctors mainly. Teachers, engineers, pilots and some journalists too. And they are all children of the very poorest families in Bangladesh, in this case living in a Dhaka slum. Their parents fight to feed them more than one meal per day. They attend a BRAC primary school, of which there are 34,000 in Bangladesh serving 5 million children, because it is free.

BRAC primary schools are only available to communities that have no access to formal education. They operate where government schools do not. They teach a curriculum that focuses on Bengali, English, maths, science and social studies – the core skills that children will require at high school and in life. These include repeated messages on gender equality, awareness of the dangers of child marriage, sexual health, hygiene and clean water. What good is learning if you cannot stay healthy to pursue your dream to be a doctor, or if you are spirited away to a marital home aged 15? All subjects are taught in a way that encourages questioning, interaction and student leadership. As a member of the education team put it, 'They are taught to argue'. As the students put it, 'It's fun'. Girls and boys are taught together, and equally. BRAC children do much better on average on standardised tests than those attending government or other NGO schools.

In most villages, BRAC schools are not established until a microfinance programme has laid the foundations for learning with the older generation. BRAC staff often refer to their work in this area as 'microfinance ++'. Certainly, it is about offering small-scale loans to individuals who would not be able to access them in the private sector. Usually, they are for income-generating activities – from buying a cow to produce and sell milk, to starting a small tea, sari or cake-making business. Loans are underpinned by training on how to manage money and accounts, and how to sign your own name and have a formal identity.

There is another kind of learning that enables microfinance beneficiaries to sustain their living – and give their children a different future. In a small village by the roadside in Gazipur, near Dhaka, a group of women sit in a circle and chant. They are repeating the '18 oaths' of the microfinance programme. Some are exactly as you would expect – a commitment to making regular loan payments, and to start saving as a

buffer against uncertainty. Others are more general – they are about a commitment to send their children to school, to boil water before they give it to their families to drink, and to the equality of men and women. Fulpori glows with pride as she introduces her tall, strong son and talks about what she has achieved. She used her loan to buy land for a rice field, some of which feeds her family, and some of which is sold at a profit. 'Before, I worked in the brick fields and my daughter worked in the garment factory. Now, my son has finished grade 12 and we hope he will go to university. My youngest daughter is in grade 3.' Her income has changed, and so have her priorities. She has a new, personal importance to the family as the primary bread-winner – and a new belief in her own value. 'Before, my husband used to beat me all the time. Now he doesn't.'

So the two programmes reinforce each other, practically and in spirit: microfinance can help families to generate a stable income so the children do not have to work and everyone can be fed; it is also the vehicle through which parents – mostly mothers – absorb the value of sending their children to school.

In these two elements of the picture, learning skills and values are intertwined. Young people are acquiring the knowledge, tools and confidence they need to get and sustain work today and in the future – they are being taught to challenge, argue and solve problems. The principles are recognisable from Chapters 3 and 4: learning is collaborative, tied to real-world challenges, and led by learners themselves. At the same time, students, their families and their communities are learning new values. They are beginning to believe that they can change things for themselves, that education matters, and that boys and girls are equal.

At BRAC University, values and creating possibilities also come hand in hand. BRAC University was founded in 2001 to fill a gap perceived by its leaders. Universities were not equipping young people to be citizens, to have the creativity and application to help reshape and rebuild the country.

BRAC University runs all of its courses in English – the basic minimum to operate at a global level. Its most distinctive requirement is that all students attend a residential semester, outside Dhaka. They take three, core courses: Bangladesh studies, culture and ethics, and English. During this semester students learn to be proud of their history, and they learn empathy with their fellow citizens. A 'social lab' day has all the students swapping roles with the staff running the campus – from security guards and cooks, to cleaners and gardeners. Each of the students spends several days on a field trip in one of BRAC's many poverty alleviation programmes, learning about people's lives. Their response is unequivocal, 'Why can't we do all our studying here… it's too short.' So is that of the university's Pro Vice Chancellor: 'We are building Bangladesh's future leaders.'

In class, BRAC shares similar approaches to 2iE, Lumiar, Big Picture Learning and others: they are discursive, project-based, and team-based. Equal attention is paid to teachers' personal experience and understanding of these modes of learning as to the students. They are the ones transmitting those values and practices, so they have to feel them.

The outcome, says BRAC University's Pro-Vice-Chancellor, is 'competent, ethically driven, responsible citizens'.

Perhaps most strikingly, BRAC very consciously learns as an organisation in the same way it encourages its members to – whether they are 5, 20 or 50. At a lively discussion with BRAC's education team, they sought to identify the principles they learn and work by:

> 'We have a collective aspiration to live better, together.'
> 'People are generous – they always attribute good ideas
> to each other.'
> 'There is a culture of "profound listening".'
> 'We don't hesitate – if we need to talk about something,
> work through it, we do it immediately.'
> 'We are always challenging each other.'
> 'We feel like we belong here – we all want to contribute
> to a better Bangladesh.'
> 'We pounce on failure to understand why things haven't worked.'
> 'We have all internalised the desire to do better, to use
> the opportunities on offer. We all want to change things.
> We feel we have to use the space to do so.'
> 'We never give up.'

These are themes that resonate up, down and across BRAC's myriad programmes – supported by 60,000 staff in Bangladesh alone and reaching millions of Bangladeshis. Matching skills, responding to complex problems and creating possibilities all build on each other. Like WANE, LoYAC and Silver Human Resource Centres, it is the values of the organisation that mobilise its powerful work.

FOLLOWING PAGES

Mayyada Abu-Jaber
with Jordan Career
Education Foundation
alumni and local leaders
from Ma'an Governorate,
at a hotel in Aqaba.

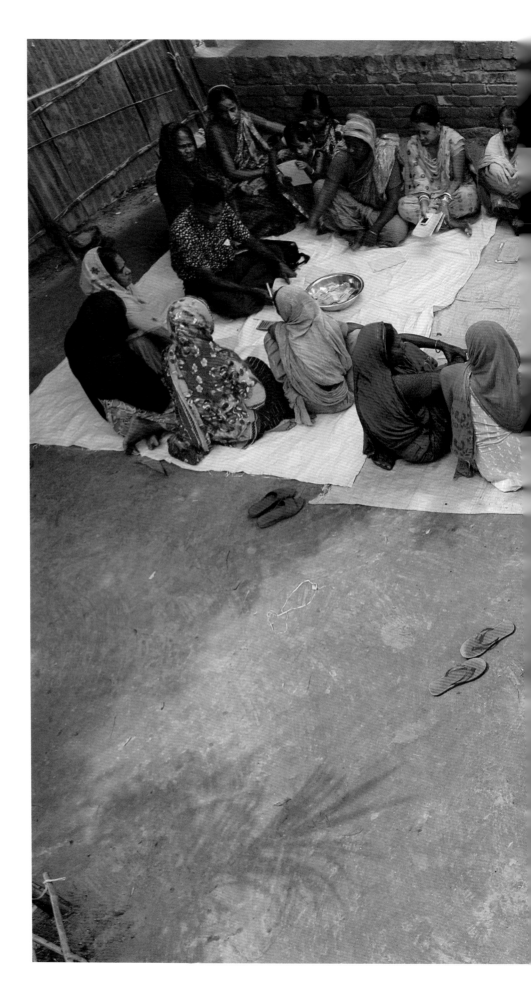

Women attending a micro-
finance meeting in Manikganj,
33 kilometres from Dhaka,
where they pay their
instalments, exchange news
and raise awareness of local
issues.

A widow and her daughter
at the 4th National Widows
Alliance Conference in Accra,
Ghana, which over
2000 widows attended.

CHAPTER 8

LEARNING A LIVING

Urgent and possible

Don't ever slow down, don't ever stop innovating.

Sir Fazle Hasan Abed
BRAC Founder and Chairperson,
and Laureate of the inaugural
WISE Prize for Education, 2011
(BRAC Bangladesh Annual Report, 2011)

LoYAC was founded by seven Kuwaiti women in response to 9/11. Big Picture Schools were founded by two outraged educators in the USA. Lumiar schools were founded in Brazil by a multimillionaire business leader, unable to recruit graduates with the right skills and attitude to work in his companies. The diversity of innovators featured in this book is matched by the diversity of contexts for innovation – from Finland with its PISA-topping education system, to post-revolution Bangladesh with its ravaged infrastructure in the 1970s. On top of that, the innovators work with learners on very different scales: from groups of hundreds, to millions. They support people to learn a living from the age of 4 to 95.

This diversity is an important finding. It is important for the striking similarities that emerge between a widows' alliance in Ghana and a not-for-profit in San Francisco. It is also important in and of itself. Leaders in this field emerge from everywhere: in different sectors, at different ages, and at different speeds.

This chapter looks at both of these angles – similarity and difference – for insights into the biggest challenge of all: what would it take for the principles and practices of these innovations to become mainstream and commonplace, for everyone to be able to 'learn a living'? Compelling stories, practice and even fully fledged learning models are

interesting, but how can we grow innovations, create more of them, and bring existing education institutions into alignment?

The similarities between cases give us powerful insights into the way we can grow existing innovations and create more of them. They tell us how to match and update skills, to learn to generate solutions and to create possibilities; *who* is likely to drive this innovation; and *what it takes to grow innovations* like these to reach the people who will benefit.

The differences offer some insights into how 'learning a living' might be brought into the mainstream – how the different routes taken by innovators, and the contexts in which they work, show us how education systems everywhere might be changed.

SIMILARITIES: HOW TO LEARN A LIVING

This diagram distils insights from throughout the book about how people learn a living. These principles are common to up-skilling time-poor farmers in Nigeria, creating world-class scientists in China and growing entrepreneurs in Nicaragua. There are four overarching points that emerge from this model.

**FROM THE CONSUMPTION OF KNOWLEDGE
TO THE PRODUCTION OF A BETTER WORLD**

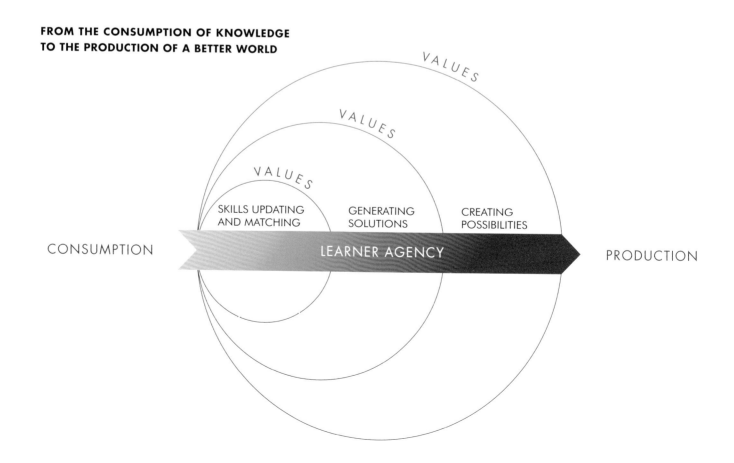

First: the role of agency. Agency is all about the ability to take control of our lives – to see, understand and act on what we believe to be important. To feel confident shaping our own future and the societies in which we live. Matching and updating skills, generating solutions to complex problems, and creating possibilities all require different levels of agency in learners – and they *generate* different levels of agency.

Acquiring a relevant, up-to-date skill base requires motivated learners to engage fully – to build their technical mastery and their ability to interact with others. They must take opportunities and actively pursue them. But as with Ahmed in JCEF, the opportunity to do something real and useful builds confidence. It grew his sense of responsibility. He is choosing now to share his knowledge with others. He is becoming an active agent of change in other people's lives as well as his own.

Generating solutions requires flexibility, creativity, and collaboration. Independence of thought and action is needed to apply knowledge and skills in new contexts. Delonda, like other young people at Rising Sun, was given the space and responsibility to exercise her problem-solving muscles 'in the field'. Doing so has built her internal sense of purpose and determination to make change happen.

Creating possibilities requires independence of thought and action. It is about seeing the world through fresh eyes and perceiving where the most important challenges and opportunities lie. It requires the courage and energy to tackle them, and to persuade others to help. Jihane, from Al Jisr School-Business Partnerships / INJAZ Al Maghrib, reflects on what it meant to receive support to start her own company: 'I found out that the more I do, the more I can do.' Agency breeds agency.

All these elements of 'learning a living' require greater levels of agency and self-responsibility than most traditional forms of learning – and they help create citizens who are capable of shaping a new world.

Second: learning principles build on each other. The diagram shows that the ways of learning that are critical for acquiring relevant skills are also the basis for generating solutions. The learning principles underpinning both of these are needed for creating possibilities. Real-world contexts are as important for building competent software engineers in India as they are for equipping young Brazilians to solve problems and for supporting young Moroccans to start new businesses. The three elements of our model build on each other. The distinctions are about emphasis and the intent of learning: focus, aspiration and opportunity – not about how people learn.

The diagram makes no distinction between academic and vocational learning. The two categories are collapsed.

Third: the model reflects the swing from 'consumption' to 'production' as we move from skills acquisition, through problem-solving, to creating possibilities.

Some economists believe that one of the major features of the emerging economy is a much more blurred line between consumption and production. It is no coincidence then that learning that attempts to equip people for the world – and to enable them to help shape it – is helping them to fill, create and redefine work.

Finally, a common emphasis on values. For these innovators, learning is not instrumental. It is playing a role in shaping societies. Values are as important as curriculum and learning methods.

SIMILARITIES: WHO

Paradoxically, the other striking similarities in this book emerge from some of its greatest contrasts – what does the 'Ghanaian Oprah' have in common with a Chinese professor? The answer lies in the energy, insight, and determination they bring to their tasks.

The innovators featured in this book are a motley crew, but each as it were with their own 'superpower', assembled from crises and dysfunctions across the globe, and united – even if they do not know it yet – by a common cause.

Their starting point is almost always the same – a very personal response to a social crisis that cannot be ignored. Dennis Littky and Elliot Washor at Big Picture talk about their rage at all the young people from the most disadvantaged backgrounds being failed dismally by the US education system – and how they could not look the other way any longer. Markus Fischer was determined that young people in rural Nicaragua would be given an opportunity to break the cycle of poverty – and that he should do something about it. Their message to aspiring innovators about how they can move from passion to impact might include the following elements.

Their approach **builds on their strengths and their insights.** Mama Zimbi understands that her most important asset is her public profile – the trust and respect in which she is held. She uses it to its full potential to do what she believes matters. All innovators are working with the grain of who they are, as well as what they observe to be important.

These innovators all **practice what they preach**. Sir Fazle Hasan Abed, chairman and founder of BRAC, the first Laureate of the WISE

Prize for Education, insists on being called 'brother' as a regular colleague would be. The WISE Prize For Education is the world's first major recognition of an outstanding contribution to education, just as there are global awards for medicine, science, literature and human rights. Sir Fazle eats the simple and cheap lunch from the staff canteen. It is exactly the way that all staff are required to interact with their users or 'members' – equally and with respect.

Every one of these innovators has **a remarkable pride of place**, a belief in what it should mean to be Nigerian, Japanese or American. They all take strength from this and use it as a beacon. 'I want to help build a better India,' says Narayana Murthy. 'I want to help drive the development of Africa,' says Paul Ginies, Director General of 2iE.

They are all extremely **rigorous in their commitment to excellence and evidence**. Conversation at BRAC is peppered with references to famous thinkers, whose insights and research help inform their work. SUSTC has recruited professors at the top of their fields from across the world. JCEF is very serious about rigorous quality assurance. Big Picture pays close attention to data on student outcomes – and learn from it.

Finally, they are all **hungry for collaboration and learning** wherever possible. This is not about being evangelical about an approach – it is about the search for partners who can help challenge, build and grow the innovation, around the kernel of its values and core.

SIMILARITIES: WHAT IT TAKES TO GROW AN INNOVATION

BRAC stands out amongst the case studies for this book as a global leader in scaling innovation. It is the largest NGO in the world. It has an annual turnover of around $650 million, reaches over 110 million people worldwide, employs 120,000 staff, runs 34,000 primary schools in Bangladesh alone and now works in more than 10 countries.

Its founder, Fazle Hasan Abed, is famous for his catchphrase, 'Small is beautiful… but big is necessary.' With its roots in the post-revolution Bangladesh of the 1970s, this thirst for scale is understandable. The country was on its knees. An estimated 28,000 people died as a result of flooding in 1974, most were starving, and life expectancy was 42. [56] To have a real impact on his country (population 150 million), Fazle Hasan Abed knew he would have to touch millions of lives.

At BRAC, growing innovation has at least two different meanings. There is depth, and breadth. Depth is about achieving maximum reach with a particular innovation – their much-lauded primary schools reach 5 million of the country's poorest children and achieve results well above average on standardised tests. Simply put, it means not resting until everyone who can be helped by an intervention has had a chance to take it.

Breadth is about identifying and responding to new and different needs. It is about starting secondary schools now that primary coverage is improving. It is, as Nnaemeka of Smallholder Farmers Rural Radio put it, where need is 'just obvious' and you can see how to do something about it.

As with the learning principles and characteristics of innovators, BRAC reveals similar messages about how to grow innovations as its smaller colleagues in Nicaragua, China, and Kuwait.

Think big, start small. At the heart of both deep and broad scale is pure ambition, the vision and determination to act big. Fazle Hasan Abed is not the only one to think that way. Mama Zimbi can see the need and is planning to work across the whole of Africa to help widows everywhere; SUSTC is working to transform China's whole economy; 2iE is working on the development of the whole African continent, so they are stimulating a market of potential competitors to help them; Omnia aspires to change VET teacher training across Finland. All of these innovators may start small by necessity, but they are thinking big from day one.

These innovators all agree that thinking big requires starting small – and rigorously testing new approaches before scaling them up. SUSTC wants to transform China's economy but is very consciously testing its learning model rigorously with 45 students. InnoOmnia has begun by prototyping new approaches to learning in one programme.

Infrastructure links 'starting small' with 'thinking big'. Growth requires back office systems and tools that can support thousands of users as well as 10. For Smallholder Farmers Rural Radio, this meant having a transmitter that could reach millions of farmers from the outset. For JCEF it meant building a good reputation with the national representatives of businesses in Jordan even when they were working with small groups of young people.

Think big, start small. Follow need. Understanding people's lives can reveal needs in unexpected places. Big Picture's work in transforming schooling revealed the need for a new kind of higher education, so they are starting College Unbound. SUSTC know where they are starting – the demand is clearly there – and know equally that where this will lead is unknown. They are all committed to the journey because the purpose is the right one. And they will all 'act where necessary', even if it is not what they anticipated at the start.

Think big, start small. Follow need. Build on local capacity, recruit for passion. Building on local capacity makes scale possible. It might be Growth Sector transforming well-subscribed community colleges in California, Lumiar using local experts to help children learn, or rural radio using community members as broadcasters. All look for and build on what or who is already there. Equally, innovators rely heavily on their teams to do bold, locally sensitive work at scale. They recruit passionate, expert, challenging people who are motivated by purpose, not by money. For key roles at BRAC, the chairman himself looks for the very best person to fill the role. He personally courted the current Managing Director and Executive Director. Many people stay for decades. Rising Sun often recruits from amongst previous programme participants. Scale relies on trust and determination – so finding the right people to do the work is key.

Think big, start small. Follow need. Build on local capacity, recruit for passion. Think global. Big Picture runs 52 schools outside the US, and is negotiating to work on other continents. Dennis Littky and Elliot Washor work abroad with systems that share their philosophy. Their constituency is defined by shared challenges, not by geography. BRAC works in 10 countries worldwide. 2iE is working with universities across the whole of Africa. Infosys offers its training programme across the globe. Thinking global is about feeling responsibility and seeing relevance to a community of need, not a nation.

Think big, start small. Follow need. Build on local capacity, recruit for passion. Think global. Be alert to supply and demand. Growing innovation carries responsibility. Generating a big supply of learners might mean helping to create demand for them. BRAC's microfinance programme supported farmers to learn better agricultural methods and buy cows. It led to an oversupply of milk in rural areas and farmers began to struggle again. But there was undersupply elsewhere – in urban areas where fewer people had cows of their own. BRAC started a social enterprise that would help transport milk safely to where it was needed. The dairy processes 29.2 million litres per year and is planning a major expansion to respond to the further expansion of local dairy farmers.

Think big, start small. Follow need. Build on local capacity, recruit for passion. Think global. Be alert to supply and demand. Develop economic resourcefulness and resilience. Economic resilience is critical to sustaining work at scale. It requires a diverse portfolio and resourcefulness. BRAC is now 70% self sufficient as an organisation. Its 16 social enterprises – from the dairy to an artificial insemination venture that trains and employs farmers – make $421 million per year. 2iE's partnerships with private companies and its spin outs do something similar. La Bastilla's eco-lodge and other enterprises have made it 60% self-sufficient so far. More is planned. Big Picture's

enterprises feed back into the schools (as in *Dollars for Scholars)* but the organisation constantly scans for new resources, thus modeling the entrepreneurialism it seeks to impart.

DIFFERENCES

Identifying similarities was about learning directly from the innovators and innovations in this book. But these commonalities could easily be misleading. This book set out to find remarkable innovations and was not disappointed. The majority are social enterprises. Does this mean that all the world really needs in order to make learning a living the norm is a lot more social entrepreneurs like Mama Zimbi, Mayyada Abu Jaber and Professor Zhu?

The sheer diversity of innovations and innovators in this book suggest not. These differences tell us that innovation can and does come from anywhere where there is insight, passion, determination and the space to act. Social entrepreneurs are often amongst the bravest and boldest in 'creating possibilities', whatever the context. Public servants and businesses can be more constrained by regulation, targets and the day job. It should not be surprising then that social enterprise is at the cutting edge. But it suggests that there are others waiting to be unleashed. So the real question is, how can more social entrepreneurs – and others – be given the space to explore and to lead?

THE EXISTING ROLES OF GOVERNMENT

Throughout the book, there are numerous examples of governments creating contexts in which innovation can flourish – some conscious, some not. At one end of the spectrum, projects like BRAC, Smallholder's Rural Radio and JCEF are responding quite simply to government failure. In the early days of BRAC, the Bangladeshi government did not have the resources to tackle poverty. BRAC filled a gap. The same is true in relation to ill-equipped farmers in Nigeria and unemployed young people in Jordan. Innovators can emerge from anywhere because there is a huge gap for them to fill and low barriers to entry. Governments have little energy or resource to regulate new entrants where they cannot act. It is the new entrants who are entirely defining the space for innovation.

In the middle of the spectrum are innovations like 2iE, Big Picture, and Rising Sun. In these cases, there is government involvement – through funding and minimum standards. 2iE and Big Picture receive government money for their contribution to a national, education agenda.

They have earned themselves the freedom to operate as they see fit by virtue of their excellent results. They have carved out the space to do things differently.

At the opposite end of the spectrum to BRAC and JCEF are Omnia in Finland and Silver Human Resource Centres in Japan. In Finland, it is the government's own desired outcomes for education that are driving innovation at Omnia – the desire for equity in the opportunities it offers its young people and indeed its older workers. In Japan, it was the government's response to a looming demographic crisis that built SHRCs – the desire to make the most of their human capital. At this end of the spectrum government is actively shaping the space for innovation.

This is as true for scaling successful innovations as it is for testing them out. BRAC has delineated areas in which it works at scale (34,000 primary schools with the poorest children) and where the government does not operate. 2iE sees scale across Africa as the aim, so it works with any governments or institutions with the desire and values to make it happen. Omnia is tendering for and winning government contracts to roll out its approach.

In all of these cases, innovators are working within government priorities, policies and standards. They are all working from a platform of sorts. The difference is that some of these springboards are springier than others. Finland is attempting to give Omnia a boost that will help it to extend its impact radically. The government of Burkina Faso is enabling 2iE to operate, but not necessarily to extend its impact. The government of Nigeria is largely unaware of and unconcerned about Smallholder Farmers Rural Radio, so it operates freely but relies on support from international organisations to scale its work.

This can be hugely frustrating. As Mhammed Andaloussi from Al Jisr School-Business Partnerships / INJAZ Al Maghrib says, 'My mission is to change, and it's urgent. I know we can spread this faster. If we partnered 50-50 with government we could franchise – but the emphasis needs to be on quality, not just numbers. It must become a part of the curriculum, not an extra-curricular add-on.'

GOVERNMENT FOR INNOVATION

So governments – consciously or not – create the platform upon which innovation can flourish, or not. Innovators are doing the best they can in all of these contexts but, in many, only the very bravest and the most driven by personal passion need apply. And progress can be slow. What would it take for government to become a platform that actively stimulated innovation from everywhere? That supported it to flourish and helped to maximise its impact at pace?

A SENSE OF MISSION

Generating a sense of mission has to be the starting point. For the innovators in this book, the driving force of mission often happened by chance – Mama Zimbi's texts from listeners, or Fareah Al Saqqaf in post-9/11 Jordan. Remarkable things have relied on the right people being in the right place at the right time. This cannot of course be guaranteed. Most of these people are giving up their lives to pursue their mission. It cannot be a recipe for a systematic, global revolution in learning.

The argument arising from this book – and the mission to be adopted – is that it is not enough for citizens to have access to education and 'training'. In order to shape a fast changing world, we need learning that matches and updates skills; grows the ability to generate solutions; and also builds the capacity to create possibilities. Underpinning these needs to be a strong emphasis on developing *agency* and *values*.

And it is urgent. This should not be a case of structural or tweaking reforms. This should be a call for transformation, at all levels.

This is as important in advanced economies as elsewhere. Hiroshi Mikitani, a Japanese entrepreneur, talks about his country's 'pleasant decline'[57]. Old norms of business and ways of learning are out of date. But there is little incentive to change. Most people live comfortably and in the short term. Japan remains amongst the most productive global economies; the same is true of many Western European economies. It is not true of 2iE in Burkina Faso or in Nicaragua. There, new sources of growth and value in the economy are a lifeline – not just an interesting development. There is an urgency that is felt, not just discussed. But a changing global economy will be urgent for all, over the next ten years. All economies need to generate a new and 'felt' sense of mission to help drive change.

Certainly, this new mission should liberate the latent social entrepreneurs. But it should also inspire teachers, businesspeople, politicians and others to take part. This broad participation is critical – and not just because it creates a bigger pool of talent and more resources. As Chapter 6 highlighted, learning a living is as much about values as it is about skills and knowledge. Values come from all around us – so this must be a shared endeavour, a wholesale cultural shift involving all groups that help shape society.

Aruba Al Own,
a LoYAC beneficiary.

Microfinance borrowers
in Manikganj, 33 kilometres
from Dhaka. The BRAC
microfinance programme
is the largest in the world.

WORKING WITH NEW ENTRANTS

This shared mission must come accompanied by a real openness to new entrants and collaboration. Government cannot 'deliver' this alone.

Governments in the Middle East and North Africa (MENA) have been jolted by the Arab Spring. They have awoken to the levels of complexity involved in addressing the problems faced by young people, and the fact that they can have no monopoly of solutions – even assuming they fully understood the problems. This has created space for a few organisations to mobilise energies and build new partnerships focused on a key characteristic: innovation. One such organisation is Silatech, an enterprise founded in Qatar by HH Sheikha Moza bint Nasser and working fluidly across the entire MENA region with a wide range of partners and alliances to create new programmes. 'The cracks had been visible for over a decade,' says Dr Tariq Yousef, CEO of Silatech, describing the background to the Arab Spring. 'The whole mindset towards youth and their future needed to change. The transition to adulthood is not being enabled effectively. Much flows from the inability of young people to find work, but that is just one part of the problem. The challenge now is how to work within a context of raised expectations.'

Dr Yousef sums it up thus: 'Everything we do has to be characterised by innovation. And this must apply in two domains: first in the arena of policy and policy-making. That is what is needed now. And we have to build new partnerships between governments, businesses, social enterprises and like-minded individuals across our countries. And we have to think and act regionally. We have to innovate the partnership process itself.'

GOVERNMENT INCENTIVES

Governments might also create incentives for this work to take place. If the triple bottom line (people, planet, profit) is fundamental to economies of the future – and should be infused throughout learning – what is the triple bottom line measure of national progress? Many have talked about 'good growth' and its indicators, from happiness to social mobility. At one level down, there is a huge question about the measures of success in new kinds of learning across the board – from standardised tests in schools, to what a degree really is, to professional qualifications.

GOVERNMENT AS BROKER

A further plank of the platform that governments might build is as a lateral broker – connecting innovators with others who complement or support their work. Not one of the innovators in this book is working in isolation. It would not be possible. Learning a living is about contributing to and shaping whole societies, which happens at the intersection between different sectors. Reeta Roy, President and Chief Executive of the Mastercard Foundation, explains it like this:

> The actors in this field are changing. It's not just about governments and education institutions, but also private sector employees, NGOs and individual innovators and entrepreneurs. Young people and their communities are most important and need to remain at the center of innovative program design. If we capitalise on that and get all actors to really listen, the design process will come alive and yield far better results.

Mastercard is not alone in its insight – companies from ExxonMobil and Unilever to Infosys and LEGO are building cross-sector partnerships to help shape the learners of the future.

FUNDING

Finally, who funds what? Learning a living is not just about schools. It is not even about formal education at all levels and ages. It is about all the learning that happens at home, at work listening to the radio, or downloading a Khan Academy video. It will happen at every level of society, throughout our lives, 'from the nursery years right up to the stratum of society inhabited by the world's top CEOs and political leaders', says John Elkington. Even the richest governments cannot fund it all. Who puts what money where to get the right mix?

It is impossible to imagine this kind of lifelong learning happening systematically, at scale, without a blend of financing. Everyone has a role, everyone benefits, everyone pays. Robin Murray describes this space as the social economy [58] – the areas where governments, markets, not-for-profits and households overlap to create new kinds of value. This is already visible in many of the innovations in this book. Rising Sun's operations are funded by private companies, government, households and a social enterprise fund. Individual students, multinationals, social enterprises and government make 2iE's work possible. They all benefit.

A CALL TO ACTION

The exact configuration of these partnerships and platforms will look very different in different areas. Different governments and societies have vastly different resources and infrastructures to draw on. But however well off the society, the worst thing that any government can do is to try to own it all. Learning a living cannot be decreed or 'delivered' – it has to be widely owned and shaped.

This is not the same as saying that governments have no role. We are talking about a major cultural shift in relation to learning: one which collapses the vocational and academic divide, prepares learners to participate in society, and gives them the power to help shape it. It is impossible for governments alone to engineer this shift, but they are critical to creating the conditions in which it can take place. It may seem risky, but staying still is infinitely more risky.

We have argued that governments can create a platform, lead a movement towards new kinds of learning, and encourage leaders from any sector to participate. They can use their levers of measurement and accountability to incentivise new behaviours and link organisations and people together. Finally, they can shift their funds from old ways of learning to new, to show others the way.

This is not a theoretical wish list. It is an immediate call for change. Learning a living is not a supplement to the curriculum. It is not secondary to 'academic' learning. Academic education is part of the process and would be changed by it. Learning a living can be a powerful engine for reform, if it is given the consideration it deserves. We should insist loudly on its transformative power.

The world is changing, and learning must change too.

Gathering of the Hipko
Widows Association at
the Gari Processing plant –
a WANE project in Volta
Region, Ghana. (Gari is made
from cassava.)

The Akwamufie Widows
Association, at the WANE
palm kernel project site,
saying goodbye to Mama
Zimbi.

NOTES

[1]   *In Their Hands.* Hannah Beech. Time Magazine China Report. June 2012

[2]   *In Their Hands.* Hannah Beech. Time Magazine China Report. June 2012

[3]   *Defining the Knowledge Economy: Knowledge Economy Programme Report.* July 2006. Ian Brinkley. The Work Foundation

[4]   *The World at Work: Jobs, Pay and Skills for 3.5 billion People.* June 2012. Richard Dobbs, Anu Madgavkar, Dominic Barton, Eric Labaye, James Manyika, Charles Roxburgh, Susan Lund, Siddarth Madhav. McKinsey Global Institute

[5]   bsr.london.edu/lbs-article/581/index.html

[6]   Gartner Press Release, 2012. *Gartner Newsroom Web Portal.* Available at: www.gartner.com/it/page.jsp?id=1416513

[7]   *Defining the Knowledge Economy: Knowledge Economy Programme Report.* July 2006. Ian Brinkley. The Work Foundation

[8]   *Greening Jobs and Skills: Labour Market Implications of Addressing Climate Change.* 2010. Cristina Martinez-Fernandez, Carlos Hinojosa, Gabriela Miranda. OECD

[9]   *Greening Jobs and Skills: Labour Market Implications of Addressing Climate Change.* 2010. Cristina Martinez-Fernandez, Carlos Hinojosa, Gabriela Miranda. OECD

[10]   *Greening Jobs and Skills: Labour Market Implications of Addressing Climate Change.* 2010. Cristina Martinez-Fernandez, Carlos Hinojosa, Gabriela Miranda. OECD

[11]   *Global Employment Trends for Youth 2012.* May 2012. International Labor Office

[12]   *The Jobless Young: Left Behind.* September 2011. The Economist

[13]   US Department of Labour Employment Situation Summary, 2012. *Bureau of Labour Statistics web portal.* www.bls.gov/news.release/empsit.nr0.htm

[14]   economywatch.nbcnews.com/_news/2012/08/02/13070977-temp-jobs-become-a-permanent-way-of-life-for-some?lite

[15]   *Youth in the Balance.* David E Bloom. Finance & Development, March 2012, Vol. 49, No. 1

[16]   United Nations Population Fund article on Population Ageing. Available at www.unfpa.org/pds/ageing.html

[17]   *Ageing Workforce: 2006 Report Asia Pacific.* 2006. Watson Wyatt

[18]   *2012 Talent Shortage Survey Research Results.* 2012. Manpower Group

[19]   *Is this the Bursting of the Education Bubble?* May 2012. Rupert Cornwell. The Independent Comment

[20]   Executive Summary of Interview with John May, World Bank Demographer, 2008. *World Bank Website Africa Pages.* web.worldbank.org/WBSITE/EXTERNAL/COUNTRIES/AFRICAEXT/0,,contentMDK:21709116~pagePK:146736~piPK:226340~theSitePK:258644,00.html

[21]   Progress on Drinking Water and Sanitation: 2012 Update. 2012. UNICEF

[22]   2iE 'Achievements and Perspectives' presentation, March 2012

[23]   Burkina Faso at a Glance. *World Bank Burkina Faso Data and Statistics Web Page* devdata.worldbank.org/AAG/bfa_aag.pdf>

[24]   Statistical Telecommunications Highlights, 2012. *International Telecommunications Union Statistics Webpage* www.itu.int/ITU-D/ict/statistics/material/pdf/2011%20Statistical%20highlights_June_2012.pdf

[25]   *Finnish Lessons: What can the world learn from educational change in Finland?* Sahlberg, P Teachers College Press 2011; *The Finland Phenomenon: Inside the World's Most Surprising School System;* Wagner T 2010 (video)

[26]   UNESCO Press Release, 2012. *UNESCO Media Services.* Available at: www.unesco.org/new/en/media-services/single-view/news/building_skills_for_work_and_life

[27]   *Pre-Employment Skills Development Strategies in the OECD,* November 2009. Yoo Jeung Joy Nam. Social Protection Unit of the World Bank

[28]   Young People Not in Employment, Education or Training. *European Commission Eurostat Webpage.* epp.eurostat.ec.europa.eu/statistics_explained/index.php/Young_people_not_in_employment,_education_or_training_-_NEET

[29]   www.oecd.org/edu/oecdskillsstrategy.htm

[30]   Bransford, J. et al *How People Learn* 2000 The National Academies Press

[31]   Labour and Social Protection, 2012. *The World Bank Data-bank.* Available at: data.worldbank.org/topic/labor-and-social-protection

[32]   *Jordan: Selected Issues.* May 2012. IMF Country Report

[33]   *College Enrollment Hits All-Time High, Fueled by Community College Surge.* October 2009. Richard Fry. Pew Research Centre

[34]   *Meet the New Boss.* April 2012. Jonathan Alter. The Atlantic

[35]   *Electricity in Africa: The Dark Continent.* August 2007. The Economist

[36]   Statistical Telecommunications Highlights, 2012. *International Telecommunications Union Statistics Webpage* www.itu.int/ITU-D/ict/statistics/material/pdf/2011%20Statistical%20highlights_June_2012.pdf

37   *Climate Change and Labour:*
The Need for a 'Just Transition'.
2010. International Journal
of Labour Research Vol 2 Issue 1.
International Labour Office

38   US Department of
Labour Employment Situation
Summary, 2012. *Bureau*
of Labour Statistics web portal.
www.bls.gov/news.release/
empsit.nr0.htm

39   Gartner Says the World
of Work Will Witness 10 Changes
during the Next 10 Years, 2012.
Gartner Webpage. www.gartner.
com/it/page.jsp?id=1416513

40   *The Power of Unreasonable*
People: How Social Entrepreneurs
Can Create Markets That
Change the World. John Elkington
and Pamela Hartigan.
Harvard Business Press 2008

41   *Reforming Chinese*
Education: What China is Trying
to Learn from America.
2012. Yong Zhao. The Solutions
Journal [online]

42   Daniel Pink, *A Whole New*
Mind: Why Right-brain Thinkers
Will Rule the World. 2005.
Daniel Pink. Riverhead Books

43   Daniel Pink, *Drive:*
The Surprising Truth About
What Motivates Us. 2009.
Daniel Pink. Riverhead Books

44   *First Generation College*
Students Stay the Course.
March 2010. Krista Ramsey
and Cliff Peale. USA Today

45   *Global Entrepreneurship*
Monitor Report 2011. 2012.
Donna J. Kelley, Slavica Singer,
Mike Herrington. Global
Entrepreneurship Monitor

46   www.worldbank.org/
en/news/2012/05/14/
challenge-of-youth-inclusion-
in-morocco

47   *Entrepreneurship in*
Primary and General Secondary
Education: National Strategies,
Curricula and Learning
Outcomes. March 2012.
Anita Bourgeois. European
Commission

48   *World Class Learners:*
Educating Creative
and Entrepreneurial Students.
Professor Yong Zhao.
Corwin Press 2012

49   *The Graduates of 2012*
will Survive only the Crack
of our Economy. 2012.
Paul Mason. *The Guardian*
– The Graduate Without
a Future Series

50   John Elkington.
Interview for this book

51   *The Craftsman.* 2008.
Richard Sennett. Penguin Books

52   Japan population
to shrink by a third by 2060.
January 2012. *The Guardian.*
Available at: www.guardian.
co.uk/world/2012/jan/30/
japan-population-shrink-third

53   Background Note: Kuwait.
2012. *US Department*
of State Country Profile Webpage.
Available at: www.state.gov/r/
pa/ei/bgn/35876.htm

54   *Learning: The Treasure*
Within. Jacques Delors.
UNESCO Publishing 1996

55   *A Better India: A Better*
World. April 2009. Narayana
Murthy. Penguin Books

56   *Unicef Statistics:*
Bangladesh. Available at
www.unicef.org/infobycountry/
bangladesh_bangladesh_
statistics.html

57   *'Hiroshi Mikitani'.*
David Pilling. *Financial Times.*
15 June 2012

58   Robin Murray –
Crisis and the Social Economy –
NESTA pamphlet

BIBLIOGRAPHY

BOOKS

A Better India: A Better World.
Narayana Murthy.
Penguin Books 2009.

Drive: The Surprising Truth About What Motivates Us. Daniel Pink.
Riverhead Books 2009.

A Whole New Mind: Why Right-Brainers will Rule the Future.
Daniel Pink.
Riverhead Books 2005.

A Whole New Mind: Why Right-Brainers will Rule the Future.
Daniel Pink. Riverhead Books
2005. *Grit: The skills for success and how they are grown.*
Yvonne Roberts.
The Young Foundation 2009.

How People Learn: Brain, Mind, Experience and School. John D.
Bransford,
Ann L. Brown and Rodney R.
Cocking (eds.).
National Academy Press 2000.

Innovation and Entrepreneurship in Developing Countries. Wim
Naude, Adam Szirmai
and Micheline Goedhuys.
United Nations University Press
2011.

Responsibility at Work: How Leading Professionals Act. Howard
Gardner. Jossey-Bass 2007.

Schooling in the Workplace: How Six of the World's Best Vocational Educational Systems Prepare Young People for Jobs and Life.
Nancy Hoffman.
Harvard Education Press,
Cambridge, MA 2011.

The Boundaryless Career: A New Employment Principle for a New Organisational Era. Michael B.
Arthur and Denise M. Rousseau.
Oxford University Press 1996.

The Craftsman. Richard Sennet.
Penguin Books 2008.

The Next Convergence: The Future of Economic Growth in a Multispeed World. Michael
Spence.
Farrar Straus Giroux 2011.

The Power of Unreasonable People: How Social Entrepreneurs Can Create Markets That Change the World. John Elkington
and Pamela Hartigan.
Harvard Business Press 2008.

The Rise of the Creative Class, and how it's transforming work, lesire, community and everyday life.
Richard Florida
Basic Books 2008.

The Seven Day Weekend.
Ricardo Semler.
Random House Books 2003.

The Shift: The Future of Work is Already Here. Lynda Gratton.
Collins 2011.

The Start-Up of You: Adapt to the Future, Invest in Yourself, and Transform Your Career. Reid Hoffman.
Random House 2012.

The Zeronauts: Breaking the Sustainability Barrier.
John Elkington.
Routledge 2012.

21st Century Skills: Learning for Life in Our Times. Bernie
Trilling and Charles Fadel.
Jossey-Bass 2009.

World Class Learners: Educating Creative and Entrepreneurial Students. Yong Zhao.
Corwin Press 2012

REPORTS

Ageing Workforce: 2006 Report Asia Pacific. 2006. Watson Wyatt.

An Economy that Works: Job Creation and America's Future. June 2011. McKinsey
Global Institute.

Better Skills, Better Jobs, Better Lives – A Strategic Approach to Skills Policies. 2012. OECD.

Climate Change and China: Technology, Market and Beyond.
2009. Dale Jiajun Wen.
Focus on the Global South.

College Enrollment Hits All-Time High, Fueled by Community College Surge. October 2009. Richard Fry.
Pew Research Centre.

Danger and Opportunity: Crisis and the Social Economy. March
2010. Robin Murray. Nesta.

Education, Globalisation and the Knowledge Economy. 2008. Phillip
Brown, Hugh Lauder and David
Ashton. Economic and Social
Research Council.

Entrepreneurship in Primary and General Secondary Education: National Strategies, Curricula and Learning Outcomes. March
2012. Anita Bourgeois. European
Commission.

Future Work Skills 2020. 2012.
Anna Davies, Devin Fidler
and Marina Gorbis. Institute
for the Future.

Global Employment Trends for Youth 2012. May 2012.
International Labor Office

Going Separate Ways? School-to-Work Transitions in the United States and Europe. 2009. OECD Social,
Employment and Migration
Working Papers. OECD.

Global Entrepreneurship Monitor Report 2011. 2012.
Donna J. Kelley, Slavica Singer,
Mike Herrington. Global
Entrepreneurship Monitor.

Good Growth: A Demos and PWC Report on Economic Wellbeing.
John Hawsworth, Nick C. Jones
and Kitty Ussher. Demos.

Greening Jobs and Skills: Labour Market Implications of Addressing Climate Change. 2010. Cristina
Martinez-Fernandez, Carlos
Hinojosa, Gabriela Miranda. OECD.

Green Jobs: Towards Decent Work in a Sustainable, Low-Carbon World. 2008. United Nations
Environment Programme.

Good Work and Our Times. 2011.
Lucy Parker and Stephen Bevan.
The Work Foundation.

Internationalisation of Higher Education in MENA: Policy Issues Associated with Skills Formation and Mobility. 2011. The World
Bank Report No:63762-MNA.
The World Bank.

How Did the Recession Affect Different Types of Workers: Evidence From 17 Middle-Income Countries. 2011. Yoonyoung Cho
and David Newhouse. The World
Bank Human Development
Network Social Protection
and Labor Unit.

More than Just Jobs: Workforce Development in a Skills-Based Economy. March 2008. OECD.

Right for the Job: Over Qualified or Under-Skilled? 2011.
OECD Social, Employment
and Migration Working Papers
No. 120. OECD.

Social Entrepreneurship: A Vehicle for Social Change and Skills Development. 2010.
Hannah McDowell. UnLtd.

Teaching and Learning 21st Century Skills: Lessons from the Learning Sciences. 2012.
Anna Rosefsky Saavedra.
The RAND Corporation.

The Economics of Knowledge: Why Education is Key for Europe's Success. 2006. Andreas
Schleicher. The Lisbon Council.

The Effect of Economic Downturns on Apprenticeships and Initial Workplace Training: A Review of the Evidence. 2009. Giorgio
Brunello. OECD.

Learning: The Treasure Within: Report to UNESCO of the International Commission on Education for the Twenty-first Century. Jacques Delors.
1996. UNESCO.

The World at Work: Jobs, Pay and Skills for 3.5 billion People. June 2012.
McKinsey Global Institute.

2012 Talent Shortage Survey Research Results. 2012.
Manpower Group.

Workforce Skills and Innovation: An Overview of Major Themes in the Literature. 2012.
Phillip Toner. OECD Directorate
for Science, Technology
and Industry.

Working Progress: How to Reconnect Young People and Organisations. 2006.
Sarah Gillinson and Duncan
O'Leary. Demos.

World of Work 2012: Better Jobs for a Better Economy.
2012. International Institute
for Labour Studies.

THE CASE STUDIES

The 15 case studies include a wide diversity of both developed and developing economies. Initially, a research exercise was conducted to identify a set of programmes that:

1. Effectively prepare people to participate successfully in an economy: commercial, market, social, domestic, public
2. Manifest a high degree of innovation in their methods, users, approaches, locations, outcomes
3. Are future-oriented, relating to the new sets of skills needed for the 21st century
4. Are holistic: attentive to the un/employment context; changing environmental needs; and also to the lives and needs of individuals
5. Have the potential be scalable, either because the principles behind them are useful, independent of context, or because the model itself is flexible and robust enough to grow.

Some 50 examples were generated, through desk research, reviews, publications and through the WISE community networks, including winners and finalists of the WISE Awards. These are listed in Appendix 2, with links. They deserve further attention, but in a book of this length, some selection needed to be made. A series of balances was struck in order to sample as wide and diverse a set of projects as possible in a book intended to have global relevance. The final set of fifteen represent a balance between:
geographical regions
target age ranges (from 4 years to 95)
levels and styles (many types of work, many forms of preparation)
a range of provider types
styles/locations: formal, informal; accredited, etc.

2iE, Burkina Faso
www.2ie-edu.org

Big Picture Learning, USA and worldwide
www.bigpicture.org

BRAC, Bangladesh and worldwide
www.brac.net/content/about-brac-bangladesh

Infosys, India
www.infosys.com/pages/index.aspx

Al Jisr School-Business Partnerships, Morocco
(Winner of 2011 WISE Award)
www.aljisr.ma

InnoOmnia, Finland
www.slideshare.net/mervijan/
innoomnia-implementing-burges-communiqu

Jordan Career Education Foundation (JCEF), Jordan
www.jcef.jo

La Bastilla Technical Agricultural School, Nicaragua
www.bastillaecolodge.com/colegio.php?lang=en

Lothan Youth Achievement Centre (LoYAC), Kuwait
www.loyac.org

Lumiar Schools, Brazil
www.lumiar.org.br/?lang=en

Rising Sun Energy Centre, California
www.risingsunenergy.org

Silver Human Resource Centres, Japan
longevity.ilcjapan.org/f_issues/0702.html

Smallholder Famers Rural Radio, Nigeria
(Winner of 2010 WISE Award)
www.smallholdersfoundation.org/index.php

South University of Science and Technology of China (SUSTC)
www.sustc.edu.cn

Widows Alliance Network (WANE), Ghana
(Winner of 2009 WISE Award)
www.wise-qatar.org/node/1120

OTHER PROJECTS MENTIONED

Centum Learning
Worldwide

Centum Learning Limited provides end-to-end training programmes and skill development solutions aimed at productivity improvement for businesses on one hand, and employability enhancement for youth on the other. The organisation originates from India's Bharti group and operates across South Asia and Africa.
www.centumlearning.com

Growth Sector
USA

Growth Sector works with a variety of partners to develop pathway opportunities for veterans, unemployed and underemployed youth and adults that will lead to college degrees and high-wage, high-growth careers.
growthsector.org

ExxonMobil Bernard Harris Summer Science Camps
USA

Two-week-long, free residential camps that offer innovative programmes to enhance student knowledge in STEM topics, while also fostering leadership and citizenship. The core curriculum is integrated with field excursions and other educational experiences to enrich students' understanding of the practical relationships between classroom work and the real world.
www.theharrisfoundation.org/sitecontent/565/summer-science-camp/category/457/education.aspx

Rubisadt Foundation
Cameroon

The RUBISADT Foundation aims to empower young women to understand global and continental challenges and to develop analytical and problem-solving skills so as to contribute to developing their nation as responsible citizens. To meet these challenges, the Foundation has developed and for the last decade successfully implemented an innovative and holistic method of learning that blends gender, science and technology, culture and ethics.
www.rubisadt.org/index.php/en/the-rubisadt-institute-school

Shodh Yatra
India

The Shodh Yatra are 'learning walks' carried out in remote parts of India. They aim to facilitate the exchange of knowledge and to unearth grassroots innovations that have emerged in remote rural communities in India.
www.sristi.org/cms/shodh_yatra1

Silatech
Qatar

Silatech operates in a number of countries in the Middle East. Its goal is to connect young people, 18–30 years old, with employment and enterprise opportunities. One of its main initiatives, the Taqeem Evaluation Fund, supports 11 small and medium-sized youth employment programmes to develop strategies for proving evidence of their impact.
www.silatech.com

Teach a Man to Fish schools
Africa, Asia, South America

A UK-based NGO, Teach a Man to Fish provides practical and financial support to schools in deprived parts of the world to help them to set up and run their own profit-making businesses. These school enterprises – from beekeeping to carpentry workshops – earn the schools money that covers facilities and teaching costs. More importantly these businesses act as a platform for students to develop entrepreneurial and practical skills, so that they graduate empowered, ready to succeed in self-employment, further education, and life.
www.teachamantofish.org.uk/

Qatar Foundation for Education,
Science and Community Development
Qatar

Qatar Foundation for Education, Science and Community Development supports the transition of Qatar from a carbon economy to one based on the development of knowledge. It was established in 1995 by His Highness the Amir of the State of Qatar Sheikh Hamad bin Khalifa Al-Thani. Her Highness Sheikha Moza bint Nasser is Qatar Foundation's Chairperson and driving force. Qatar Foundation structures its actions around three pillars: Education, Science and Research, and Community Development.
www.qf.org.qa

WISE-Qatar

WISE is dedicated to building the future of education through innovation. This global collaborative initiative was inaugurated in 2009 by Qatar Foundation under the leadership of Her Highness Sheikha Moza bint Nasser. Its mission is to address the challenges facing 21st-century education, to expand dialogue around the world and to implement practical and sustainable solutions. WISE holds an annual international Summit that is a meeting place for thought leaders and experts to share best practices in education. WISE is also a continuing initiative devoted to reaching outside the traditional circles of the education community to promote innovation and implement concrete actions.
www.wise-qatar.org

PROJECTS NOT MENTIONED BUT OF INTEREST

Aalto University
Finland
Aalto University aims to be an interdisciplinary university capable of generating innovative thought. It runs a series of multidisciplinary workshops called Aalto Factories, designed to facilitate new forms of collaboration in an environment where academic teams, researchers and students work together with companies and communities.
www.aalto.fi/en

The Academy (National Bank of Australia)
Australia
The National Bank of Australia has created an in-house Academy that uses a mix of online learning sites and virtual learning and collaboration technologies to further develop its employees' skills and leadership abilities. It has integrated a range of learning programmes, courses, tools and technologies so staff can better learn, share knowledge and network.
www.nab.com.au/wps/wcm/connect/nab/Careers/home/1/2/2/

Apps for Good
UK
The Apps for Good programme, run in 40 schools across the UK, takes students through a kind of entrepreneurial process whereby they identify what is wrong with their world before designing a way of fixing it with a mobile app. The programme combines a broad range of areas in the course, giving young people a foundation in entrepreneurship, community involvement, problem-solving and teamwork.
appsforgood.org

BBC Janala *(Winner of a 2011 WISE Award)*
Bangladesh
BBC Janala uses mobile, web, television and print media to enable millions of people in Bangladesh to learn English in a simple and affordable way. It is the largest multi-platform innovation to improve English language skills anywhere in the developing world.
www.bbcjanala.com

The Business Place
South Africa, Botswana, Swaziland
A network of drop-in business support centres that offer support to entrepreneurs by providing assistance with information, referrals, training, coaching, workshops, networking and business opportunities.
www.tbp.co.za

CAMFED Business Training and Microfinance
Zimbabwe, Zambia, Ghana, Malawi and Tanzania
Camfed offers training, peer support, grants and microloans to help young, predominantly rural women learn economic skills and launch small businesses.
www.camfed.org

Conexao
Brazil
Conexao is a Brazilian NGO that helps underprivileged youth to develop skills for the job market through professional training, mentorship and labour market guidance. Through it, private sector businesses can offer pro-bono consulting services to micro-entrepreneurs to strengthen their enterprises and their surrounding communities.
www.conexao.org.br/english

Cristo Rey Network *(Winner of a 2012 WISE Award)*
USA
At Cristo Rey Network schools, every student works five full days per month to fund the majority of his or her education. Students gain job experience, grow in self-confidence and are able to make connections from the classroom to the world of work.
www.cristoreynetwork.org

Daimler-Benz Apprentice Programme
Germany
The Daimler-Benz Apprenticeship Programme has existed for over 100 years and today offers training in 22 technical and 14 commercial disciplines, with 9 out of 10 trainees landing permanent jobs. Training plans for apprentices are delivered after close consultation between future employers, educators and the government.
www.emercedesbenz.com/autos/mercedes-benz/corporate-news/mercedes-benz-apprentice-training-a-top-priority-since-1890

EARTH University
Costa Rica
EARTH University is a non-profit higher educational institution that aims to prepare young people from a variety of backgrounds to contribute to the sustainable development of their countries. Its curriculum is founded on the precepts of entrepreneurship, environmental and social consciousness, ethical values, and scientific and technical knowledge.
www.earth.ac.cr

El Sistema
Venezuela

El Sistema is a publicly financed music education programme that uses music to train and rehabilitate young people, and to prevent criminal behaviour. Participation is free for all students and the programme emphasises intensive ensemble participation, group learning and peer teaching from the earliest stages.
elsistemausa.org/el-sistema/venezuela

Ethiopian Women's Leadership Programme
Ethiopia

Female students are exposed to a nine-month academic year programme that includes an internship and service learning component to help build leadership skills and assertiveness, the lack of which heavily contributes to extremely high dropout rates.
www.iie.org/en/Programs/Ethiopian-Womens-Leadership-Program

Ford International Fellowship Programme
Africa, the Middle East, Asia, Russia and Latin America

Ford's IFP provides fellowships for post-graduate study to emerging leaders from marginalised and excluded communities in Africa, the Middle East, Asia, Russia and Latin America. It seeks to empower individual social change-makers with the tools to have a significant impact in their home countries.
www.fordifp.net

High Tech High
San Diego, USA

High Tech High consists of a group of 11 public charter schools with a focus on project-based learning and adult world engagement. Teachers work in multidisciplinary teams and are given planning time to develop extended projects that combine 'academic' and 'practical' work. Older students have the chance to work on projects that engage with local topics and also complete semester-long internships with local businesses or agencies.
www.hightechhigh.org

Instituto de Educação Superior de Brasília (IESB)
Brazil

The IESB is a higher education institution that applies pedagogical principles to the development of young people. Students are in charge of their own learning experiences and the curriculum is centred on problem-solving with the aim of preparing students for the world of work.
iesb.br

Integrating Career Awareness into the ABE & ESOL classroom (SABES)
USA

SABES is a curriculum that covers the complete career-planning process in depth so that learners can get a full range of skills and an understanding of what they need to pursue career goals. It specifically focuses on helping those from a range of cultural backgrounds to understand the cultural context for seeking work in the USA.
sabes.org

Kilometro Rosso
Italy

Kilometro Rosso is a science and technology park that promotes cross-sector interaction and collaborative ways of working. It encourages cooperation and specialization with a focus on a multidisciplinary approach so as to explore the frontiers of science and technology.
www.kilometrorosso.com

King Abdullah University of Science and Technology (KAUST)
Saudi Arabia

KAUST is a graduate-only university that focuses on advancing science and technology through bold and collaborative research. KAUST admits students to engage in research in one of only three fields: energy, food and water – all deemed to be pressing global problems.
www.kaust.edu.sa

Koç 'Vocational Education:
A Crucial Matter for the Nation' project
Turkey

Initiated by the Koç Group and Turkey's Ministry of Education, this project aims to build awareness and improve vocational education by providing high school students with scholarships, internships, and priority in employment and coaching. It has led to a 68 percent increase in the number of vocational high school students, and the integration of its school-workplace cooperation model into public policy.
www.koc.com.tr/en-us/Corporate_Social_Responsibility/Holding_Activities/Pages/Education.aspx

LEGO Education
Denmark

LEGO Education develops educational solutions to help the development of children's creative, problem-solving and teamwork abilities. It offers creative pre-school activities to excite students about STEM topics, as well as the creation of education innovation centres to encourage whole-community learning.
www.legoeducation.us

Mozilla's Open Badges Project
Worldwide

This project works to recognise the skills and achievements that people gain outside of formal academic contexts, by developing technology that enables any organisation to issue, earn and display badges across the web. Learners and users can collect badges from different sources and display them through a variety of mediums, thereby leading to jobs, community recognition and new learning opportunities.
www.openbadges.org

NIIT Yuva Star Career Development Centres
India

The NIIT Yuva Star project is designed to empower and mainstream India's marginalised youth through training in communication and employability skills. The programme has expanded to 24 centres, and over 75 percent of eligible students have been placed in jobs.
www.niit.com/newsandevents/Lists/NIIT%20News/disformCustomv3.aspx?List=a325a1cf-a064-4573-b17a-3ce893a0d178&ID=163

Pixar University
USA

In order to attract and retain quality employees, Pixar conducts three-month courses for new and existing animators. The company opens up the courses to all members of staff who are expected to devote four hours every week to their own learning in new ways of 'thinking' and 'doing', and create a culture of learning.
www.youtube.com/watch?v=QhXJe8ANws8

Professional Automotive Training Centre (PATC)
USA

PATC aims to integrate education with hands-on workplace experience to provide students with the fundamental skills to succeed in the automotive industry. Students are sponsored by a local automobile dealership and conduct paid internships to integrate their learning and further develop their skills in service technology.
patc.biz

Saudi Aramco Entrepreneurship Center Company Ltd
Saudi Arabia

Saudi Aramco founded an entrepreneurship centre intending to be a major financer and incubator of new businesses in Saudi Arabia. It looks to generate job opportunities for Saudis and contribute to spreading a culture of entrepreneurship, as well as help introduce an entrepreneurial eco-system.
www.saudiaramco.com/en/home.html#news%257C%252Fen%2 52Fhome%252Fnews%252Flatest-news%252F2011%252Fwa_ed- -boosting-the-economy.baseajax.html

School for Social Entrepreneurs
UK, Canada, Australia

The School for Social Entrepreneurs supports social entrepreneurs from all backgrounds to transform their talent into real social outcomes, in the form of sustainable solutions to poverty and disadvantage in communities. It does this through the use of action-learning based programmes of personal and organisational development, as well as peer-to-peer coaching.
www.the-sse.org

Scientifically Tailored Employability Programme
India

STEP is an end-to-end 'livelihood through skills' training programme that helps underprivileged young people. Working with both government and private providers, it offers a training program designed to comprehensively enhance students' communication and soft skills, computer skills and trade-specific domain skills.
www.technable.in

Siemens AG
Germany

Siemens offers a variety of technical apprenticeships combining off-the-job college training and on-the-job work experience aimed at school leavers who want to 'earn as they learn'. The programme was launched in 2005 to further improve employees' skills in order to enhance financial and commercial capability within the company.
www.thetimes100.co.uk/downloads/siemens/siemens_13_full.pdf

SIFE
Worldwide

SIFE is a non-profit organisation that works with business and higher education to mobilise university students to make a difference in their communities while developing the skills to become socially responsible business leaders. Participating students form teams on their university campuses and apply business concepts to develop outreach projects that improve the quality of life and standard of living for people in need.
www.sife.org

SENA
Colombia

SENA is a national training service established to make Colombia more competitive in global markets. SENA's main goal is to provide high-quality education to workers, but it also aims to promote economic growth through technical support to companies and by backing innovative projects.
www.sena.edu.co/portal

Start-up Chile
Chile

Financed by the Chilean government, this programme seeks to attract early-stage, high-potential entrepreneurs to bootstrap their start-ups in Chile, and use it as a platform to expand globally. Its end goal is to convert Chile into the definitive innovation and entrepreneurial hub of Latin America.
startupchile.org

Sustainable South Bronx
USA

Sustainable South Bronx is an environmental justice organisation whose goal is to provide young people from at-risk backgrounds with meaningful opportunities to develop skills and jobs in the green economy. Their biggest programme, the Bronx Environmental Stewardship Training Program, provides free green-collar job training for the people from the most at-risk parts of the South Bronx.
www.ssbx.org

Tenaris University
Argentina

Tenaris University is a corporate university where internal experts recruited from within the company serve as the main body of instructors. The university not only encompasses training but all aspects of knowledge management, including defining and implementing different learning methods and coordinating other company initiatives in the field of education.
www.tenaris.com/TenarisUniversity.aspx

THINK Global School
USA

THINK Global School is a high school that seeks to provide students with an international experience. Students immerse themselves in 12 world cities over 12 trimesters, and the programme emphasises curriculum-linked field research, guest lectures and workshops in each host city.
http://thinkglobalschool.org

Tiimiakatemia (Team Academy)
Finland

Tiimiakatemia is the entrepreneurial school of JAMK University. Its students are organised into teams and each team runs its own cooperative businesses with the goal of learning entrepreneurial skills through real-life experience. Once they have graduated, each student embarks on a trip around the world with the money made in their businesses during their studies.
www.tiimiakatemia.fi/en

Working Rite
Scotland, UK

Working Rite is a social enterprise that sets up and delivers work-based mentoring and learning projects. The focus is on the workplace, primarily the building trades. Through an incentives system, opportunities are created for young men to be matched with a local tradesman. Trainer and trainee effectively enter into a 'deal', with the trainee completing a six-month work placement.
www.workingrite.co.uk

INDEX

Lucas Aspesi Quintiliano at the Lumiar school, São Paolo, where multi-disciplinary learning helps students to develop creativity.